The Book of ACTS

Shield Bible Study Series

WALTER M. DUNNETT

BAKER BOOK HOUSE
Grand Rapids, Michigan 49506

Contents

Preface

The traditional title, "The Acts of the Apostles," known as far back as the prologue to Luke (written about A.D. 160–180 and called the anti-Marcionite prologue), may well give way to a more generally descriptive title: "The Acts of the Holy Spirit." Through human instruments the power of God was released into the world. This power was a result of men and women being filled with the Spirit and bearing witness to their vital experiences with the now-risen Lord.

Christ promised the Holy Spirit to the disciples; He would come to dwell within the disciples; and through them He would reach out to the uttermost part of earth.

The Book of Acts is the second part of Luke's two-volume work about the rise of Christianity. In all, a total of about sixty-five years is involved—thirty to thirty-five recording the story of the life of Jesus Christ, and about thirty telling the story of the spread of the gospel (the good news about Jesus) from Jerusalem to Rome. Thus Luke and Acts together tell this exciting story.

In many respects the content of Acts is unique. We have no other primary sources for much of what is contained there. The fragmentary data which might be collected from, for example, the epistles of Paul, relating to his missionary travels and preaching, would hardly replace the detailed framework found in Acts.

One of the valuable aspects of this data is the information we have concerning the two most notable apostles: Peter and Paul. Notice, for example, that the name of one (or occasionally both) of these men occurs in all but one chapter in the book. Peter dominates chapters 1–12, while Paul is the major figure in chapters 13–28.

Acts is basically the narrative of Christian missions. According to the pattern enunciated by Christ in 1:8, the good news

8 The Book of **ACTS**

went out from Jerusalem. The sequence is fairly clear. Notice the steps listed below.

Introduction (1:1–11) The promise, the power, and the pattern

Beginnings (1:12—8:3) The gospel in Jerusalem; Peter and Stephen

Transition (8:4—11:18) The gospel in Judea and Samaria; Philip, Saul, and Peter

Expansion (11:19—21:14) The gospel in the Gentile world; Barnabas, Paul, John Mark, Silas, and Timothy

Imprisonment (21:15—28:31) The gospel in Jerusalem, Caesarea, and Rome; Paul

One must remember, however, that the steps of progress involved crossing long-standing cultural barriers—religious and social obstacles faced those who made the transition. Yet many people were willing to do so. Jews, Samaritans, and Gentiles (non-Jews) were all represented here, and the gospel was meant for them all. The salvation of God was sent as "a light for revelation to the Gentiles, And the glory of Thy people Israel" (Luke 2:32).

As Luke wrote he provided a dual framework for his message: a geographical factor and a biographical factor. He was concerned with placing the events of the Christian mission within geography. This is a way of showing that these things happened in certain identifiable places. Christianity arose within human history. It was within time and space. Luke also included important persons and the roles which they played in the great drama—a drama having cosmic implications.

Not without good reason do we see Peter in Jerusalem, Philip the evangelist in Samaria, and Barnabas and Paul in the Gentile world (beginning in Syrian Antioch). These men were divinely prepared and appointed to these major areas of ministry (see, e.g., Acts 9:15; Gal. 1:15–16; 2:7–8). By personality, culture, and attitudes, each was best suited to the peculiar task at hand. This was no coincidence, no accident of history. Even as it was with

Moses and Jeremiah, who had been prepared from birth, and into whose mouths God had placed His message for a particular situation, so it was with His messengers in these days of the early church.

We must be aware of yet one more thing. This book emphasizes the Spirit of God expressing Himself through people. Today we must be satisfied with no less. We might paraphrase the psalmist, "Unless the Spirit builds the house, they labor in vain who build it" (127:1). Unless He is the architect of our lives, we labor in vain.

The famed missionary Roland Allen, in *The Ministry of the Spirit*, writes: "We must, then, read Acts as men who believe in the gift of the Holy Ghost. If we are willing to do that, then it is plain that in the acts of the apostles we shall find a revelation of the Holy Ghost; for we shall certainly learn something of the Spirit in studying words and deeds which were the direct results of His coming into the hearts of those who so spoke and acted."[1]

Sola gloria Dei!

1. (Grand Rapids: Eerdmans, 1962), p. 12.

Themes: miracles

Outline of the Book of Acts

I. Introduction: The Apostolic Commission Given (1:1–11)

V. 1. Luke summarized the contents of his Gospel in these opening words. He had addressed the story of Jesus' life—"all that Jesus began to do and teach"—to his friend Theophilus (cf. Luke 1:1–4).

The writings of Luke alone among the Gospels were addressed to an individual. Of Theophilus we know little. His name means "loved of God" or "dear to God," and his title, "most excellent" (Luke 1:3), may indicate a man of official Roman rank (see Acts 24:2 of Felix, and 26:25 of Festus, both Roman procurators of Judea). Theophilus had been instructed already in the story of Jesus; Luke's desire was to add an orderly account for him.

V. 2. Jesus had instructed His disciples during the forty days between His resurrection and ascension. According to Luke 24:44–49, He had expounded on the Scriptures, and showed how they had prophesied His death, resurrection, and the proclamation of the good news to all nations. Too, He had promised to send the Holy Spirit: the disciples were to wait in Jerusalem for the fulfillment of His words.

V. 3. Luke added that the Lord showed Himself alive and gave many "convincing proofs" that He was indeed alive. This interesting expression (translating the single Greek word *tekmēriois*) is used by Aristotle as "a compelling sign" and by the Greek physician Galen as "demonstrative evidence." In both cases it is contrasted with imaginative or mystical assertions. For a number of these proofs, see Luke 24, where He appeared to many persons under many different circumstances (cf. I Cor. 15:5–7; I John 1:1–2). These appeals were to sensory perception and personal experience, and were confirmations of His own predictions of His resurrection (Luke 9:22; 18:31–33).

During these days Christ discoursed of "the things concerning the kingdom of God." This crucial theme had appeared often during His ministry ("kingdom" occurs at least 124 times in the Gospels), and both opens (1:3) and closes (28:31) Acts. The subject was propounded to Samaritans (8:12) and Gentiles (14:21–22; 20:25) as well as to Jews (19:8; 28:23).

Thus, in the appearance of Jesus Christ, was declared the coming of God's sovereign rule among men, and entrance into this new relationship was by faith in the Son who came to bring men into life (John 3:3; Acts 8:12; 20:21, 25). There was also a coming of God's kingdom in the future, a kingdom heralded by the appearance of the Son of man in great glory. That aspect left a number of questions in men's minds (see v. 6).

Vv. 4–5: The initial, historical fulfillment of the promise of the Holy Spirit was to take place at Jerusalem, the place in which God had placed His name. Thus the disciples were to remain there (cf. Luke 24:49).

Luke combined a usual Johannine term, "the Father" (John 14:16), with a common Pauline term, "promise" (cf. Gal. 3:14; Eph. 1:13). Together with the expression by Peter, "having received from the Father the promise of the Holy Spirit" (Acts 2:33), the words mark the primitive and authentic character of Luke's message.

John the Baptist's message is repeated (v. 5). The theme of being "baptized with the Holy Spirit" occurs four times in the Gospels (Matt. 3:11; Mark 1:8; Luke 3:16; John 1:33), twice in Acts (1:5; 11:16) and once in Paul's letters (I Cor. 12:13). Thus it was anticipated, realized, and explained, respectively. By this act God showed He accepts people of diverse origins (Jews or Gentiles) into one new entity—the body of Christ (see also 2:1–4).

V. 6. At the final meeting between Jesus and His disciples, the question uppermost in the disciples' minds concerned the time of the restoration of the kingdom to Israel. Thus the two main issues were the *time* and the *place* of its manifestation. Based on statements from the Old Testament, together with the noncanonical, intertestamental Jewish literature (preserved in the Apocrypha and the Pseudepigrapha), the Jews anticipated the coming of a literal, political kingdom, ushered in by divine intervention.[1]

---

1. See Luke 17:20–21, and the question of the Pharisees as to when the kingdom of God was coming. N. Geldenhuys, *Commentary on the Gospel of Luke* (Grand Rapids: Eerdmans, 1951), p. 440, states there was no question more burning, especially to the Pharisees, as to the time when the Messiah would bring in the kingdom of God.

Recall, too, that Jesus had announced the kingdom as "at hand" (Mark 1:15) and had taught His disciples to pray, "Father . . . Thy kingdom come" (Luke 11:2). The disciples' eager question reflected the crisis nature of the advent of the kingdom for the Jews themselves, and the requirements for those who aspired to a place in it.[2]

V. 7. Jesus' reply was a rebuke to the disciples' understanding of the issue and their aspirations for positions of rulership. Their concern was to be with other matters of great moment. The time involved and the crucial events related to the coming of the kingdom are within God's knowledge. Only as He revealed them could those events be known. Following Pentecost the disciples' understanding would be righted. They would proclaim first of all a spiritual kingdom, calling men to repentance of their sins and faith in the Redeemer. The "times of refreshing" and the coming of the appointed Messiah (Acts 3:19–20) would follow at the moment of God's timing.

V. 8. The word "but" (*alla*, an adversative particle, stronger than *de*, indicating a direct contrast to what precedes) showed a new concern for the disciples. Rather than disputing about time and position, they were to be empowered witnesses of the good news about Jesus.

First, the disciples were to receive "power" (*dynamis*), the dynamic of the Holy Spirit. Second, they were to be His "witnesses," telling of their experiences with Jesus (see Acts 4:19–20). Third, they were to proclaim the message to the world ("to the end of the earth").[3]

These men stood in a unique relation to Jesus—they had *seen* Him. This element is frequently cited: they had witnessed (with their own eyes) the risen Lord (Acts 1:22; 2:32; 3:15; 5:32; 10:39, 41; 13:31; 22:15; 26:16; cf. I Cor. 9:1; 15:5–8).

2. George F. Moore, *Judaism* (Cambridge, MA: Harvard University Press, 1958) II, 374. See also Matthew 19:28; 20:20–21; Luke 9:46; 22:24.

3. Many scholars take the immediate reference to be Rome (or, at least, the western end of the Mediterranean). In the Psalms of Solomon 8:16 (dated in the first century B.C. by R. H. Charles), "the end of the earth" probably refers to Rome. See further F. F. Bruce, *The Acts of the Apostles* (Grand Rapids: Eerdmans, 1951), p. 71; R. B. Rackham, *The Acts of the Apostles* (London: Methuen, 1901), p. 8. As far as Luke was concerned, Rome was the climax of the missionary outreach of the early church.

Now the message was to be spread across the Roman world. Luke's record makes it plain that by the Spirit's empowering alone this task could be and was accomplished.[4] Recall how frequently the apostles were weak or unable to witness for Christ during His earthly ministry. James and John once wished to destroy certain Samaritans (Luke 9:54); the disciples were unable to cast out an evil spirit (Mark 9:18); Peter denied the Lord (Luke 22:54–62); upon His arrest all the disciples fled (Mark 14:50).

Boldness of speech (Acts 4:13, 31) and great wisdom (Acts 6:3, 10) characterized the people following the coming of the Spirit upon them. While Peter was the chief spokesman for the group, the disciples generally were involved in a dedicated effort to evangelize their world.

Vv. 9–11. The final narrative in Luke's Gospel (24:50–53) is recounted: Jesus ascended to heaven. He took His place at the right hand of the Majesty on high (Heb. 1:3; 8:1; 10:12; 12:2). By means of a cloud He was taken out of the disciples' sight. Rackham has put it pointedly: "In the Old Testament the incomprehensibleness of the divine nature was typified by a cloud which hid JEHOVAH from human view: so now the human body of Jesus is concealed by the same cloud which is the cloud of the Shekinah or divine glory. He is now 'in glory'."[5]

Jesus' departure was followed by the promise of His return "in just the same way." So He had promised to return for His disciples (John 14:1–3; cf. Acts 3:20; 10:42). But while He was gone they were not to stand gazing into the sky. That was still a wrong perspective. The commission to witness to the end of the earth would not be fulfilled by gazers but by goers.

---

4. The *dynamis* is "that supernatural power by which miracles . . . were wrought and the preaching made effective," Bruce, *Acts of the Apostles*, p. 71.

5. Rackham, *Acts of the Apostles*, p. 8. This word may commend itself to the reader above that of Charles D. Willis, *End of Days 1971–2001: An Eschatological Study* (New York: Exposition Press, 1972), p. 44, who says that Jesus may have left this world "in some type of magneto-dynamic spaceship" and will return the same way (Mark 13:26; Rev. 1:7).

II. Beginnings: In Jerusalem (1:12—8:3)

As Jesus had said, the disciples' witness was to begin in Jerusalem. The first stage of development, then, was confined to this geographical area. The main characters were Peter and Stephen, and there was a variety of activity: Peter appeared as an administrator, preacher, miracle worker, defender, and disciplinarian; while Stephen, first appointed as a kind of social worker, was featured as an apologist and the first martyr in the church.

A. The Ministry of Peter Begun (1:12—5:42)

1. The choice of Matthias (1:12–26)

Two meetings are recorded in this paragraph: a prayer meeting (vv. 12–14) and a business meeting (vv. 15–26).

a. The prayer meeting (1:12–14)

V. 13. The final list of the apostles, minus Judas Iscariot, is given here (see Matt. 10:2–4; Mark 3:16–19; Luke 6:14–16). Following this point their names disappear from the record, except for references to Peter, and some incidental references to John and James, sons of Zebedee (3:1, 11; 4:13; 8:14; 12:2).

V. 14. Luke emphasized the unity of the group—all with "one mind." Of the eleven New Testament uses of the words (homothymadon), ten occur in Acts.[6] With reference to the early church, the term indicates the inner unity of a group engaged in similar actions. Their inner tensions were overcome as the community gave itself to honoring one Lord.[7]

Added to this, the believers "were continually devoting themselves" to prayer. More often than not this expression is linked with prayer (see further Acts 2:42, 46; 6:4), together with certain other activities. Paul used the words also (Rom. 12:12; 13:6; Col.

---

6. See 1:14; 2:46; 4:24; 5:12; 7:57; 8:6; 12:20; 15:25; 18:12; 19:29; Romans 15:6.
7. H. W. Heidland in *Theological Dictionary of the New Testament*, G. Friedrich, ed. (Grand Rapids: Eerdmans, 1967), V, 185, 186 (hereafter cited as *TDNT*).

4:2).[8] Here we discern one of the essential reasons for the power and spiritual accomplishments of these early believers. They laid hold on God continually. Missionary leader Peter Deyneka often has said publicly: "Much prayer, much power; little prayer, little power."

Luke also noted that Jesus' family, namely, His mother and brothers, was in attendance. This indicated a drastic change in their attitudes (see Mark 3:21, 32; John 7:5). The reversal may be laid to Jesus' postresurrection appearance to James (I Cor. 15:7). The sight of the risen Lord may have been the decisive factor.

b. The business meeting (1:15–26)

V. 15. Once more Peter assumed leadership, as he had done so often. Despite his lapse (denying His Lord), Peter had been restored (John 21:15–22). Now, instead of 12, there were 120 believers making up the community (see further I Cor. 15:6).

Vv. 16–20. Peter began to speak about Judas Iscariot. Judas' defection and death were no accident of history; rather, the Scripture had predicted that which had been fulfilled (see v. 20). Notice the important description of the sacred writing: "the Holy Spirit foretold by the mouth of David." The divine and the human elements combined to produce the record (cf. I Cor. 2:13; II Peter 1:20–21).

Judas chose his own role—he became a guide[9] to the persons arresting Jesus—and his own fate. He forfeited the opportunity which was given him by Jesus. From our Lord's description of him in John 17:12, "the son of perdition," it seems unlikely that he was truly committed to Christ (see also Matt. 26:14–16; 27:3–5; John 6:70–71; 12:4–6; 13:26–30; 18:2–3, 5).

The circumstances of Judas' death are recorded in two accounts: Matthew 27:5, "he hanged himself," and Acts 1:18, "fall-

---

8. Of the ten times this verb occurs in the New Testament, five references are related to prayer (see also Mark 3:9; Acts 8:13; 10:7). In all these passages about prayers (in Acts, as well as in Paul's letters), the definite article always occurs with the word *prayer*—"the prayer[s]." This may indicate appointed prayers, either in the upper room, or wherever the apostles met, as in the temple (3:1).

9. The same root word for "guide" occurs in John 16:13, which says the Holy Spirit "will guide" the disciples into all the truth. What a contrast with Judas!

ing headlong. . . ." While more is not known about the circumstances, one of the earliest explanations was given in a version which St. Augustine quoted: "he hanged himself and falling headlong on his face (through the rope breaking) he burst asunder in the midst."[10] Because of this bloody end of the traitor, the field which he had purchased was named the Field of Blood.

Vv. 21–22. Another apostle was to be appointed, and Peter set out the requirements: this apostle must be one who had heard Jesus' teachings and had seen His works, and had seen Him as risen Lord. The latter qualification was essential, according to Peter, for the one chosen must be able to say he had witnessed Him alive (see further 2:32; 3:15; 5:32; cf. I Cor. 9:1; 15:1–8). Furthermore, this was necessitated by the word of Scripture: "His office let another man take" (v. 20).[11]

V. 23. The two men nominated for the office are mentioned here only; after this incident their names occur no more in Acts. This has led some scholars (e.g., G. Campbell Morgan) to contend that this was a mistake on the part of the Eleven. Morgan argued that Paul was to have been the twelfth apostle. Yet it is notable that only three of the twelve are mentioned in Acts after 1:13, namely, Peter, John, and James, and the latter two only incidentally. Further, it is unlikely that Paul would have consented to such an idea (see I Cor. 15:8–9; II Cor. 12:11; Eph. 3:8). It may be significant that "Matthias" probably means "gift of Jehovah."

Vv. 24–26. While the apostles have been criticized for using lots to determine the successor to Judas, the following should be noted. First, the apostles prayed, asking the Lord to show which man He had chosen. Second, in drawing lots they used a process that was standard in Jewish life (see, e.g., Josh. 14:2; Neh. 10:34; 11:1; and especially Prov. 16:33: "The lot is cast into the lap, But its every decision is from the LORD"). Third,

10. Translated by Rackham, *Acts of the Apostles*, p. 12. See a discussion of views in R. J. Knowling, "The Acts of the Apostles" in *The Expositor's Greek Testament* (New York: Dodd, Mead and Co., 1900), II, 64–65.

11. Other references to Judas fulfilling prophetic statements occur in Matthew 27:9–10; John 13:18; and John 17:12. John used this formula: "that the Scripture may [or, might] be fulfilled."

this method is not mentioned again in the New Testament, suggesting that after Pentecost the Holy Spirit gave direction by other means.

2. The day of Pentecost (2)

In the Jewish calendar an important harvest festival occurred fifty days after the Passover celebration (thus the name *Pentecost*—literally, "the fiftieth day").[12] In the Christian church it is called Whitsunday.

On this day, as Jesus had promised (Luke 24:49; Acts 1:5), the disciples experienced the descent of the Holy Spirit. This resulted in unusual phenomena being manifested; Peter's notable speech concerning the event and its importance; and the conversion of three thousand persons in Jerusalem, a group comprising the new people of God. Perhaps the following analysis will be helpful in examining the passage: the coming of the Spirit (vv. 1–4); the reaction of the audience (vv. 5–13); Peter's speech (vv. 14–36), consisting of explanatory (vv. 14–21) and evangelistic (vv. 22–36) material; Peter's appeal (vv. 37–41); and a description of life in the early church (vv. 42–47).

a. The coming of the Spirit (2:1–4)

V. 1. The day of Pentecost, according to Jewish tradition, was the anniversary of the giving of the law at Sinai. Luke recorded the giving of the Holy Spirit on this day, making it notable to Christians.

This festival commemorated the goodness of God in giving food to the Israelites (cf. Deut. 16:10: "The LORD your God blesses you"); at this point it became a fulfillment of our Lord's promise of the living water (John 7:37–39). From these who received His gift would flow a life-giving message to all who were spiritually thirsty.

Vv. 2–4. Observe the three signs accompanying the descent of the Holy Spirit: wind, fire, and tongues. The first two are stated as literary similes: "like a . . . wind" and "as of fire," probably indicating supernatural rather than simply natural

12. See Exodus 23:16, "the Feast of the Harvest of the first fruits"; Leviticus 23:15–21.

phenomena.[13] To relate "wind" to the Spirit, see Ezekiel 37:9, 14 and John 3:8; for "fire," see Matthew 3:11. Notice also Elijah's experience in I Kings 19:11–13, in which wind, fire, and a voice occurred.

Upon being filled with the Holy Spirit, the disciples began to speak in languages other than their own (see v. 8); thus their hearers understood their words (v. 11). The miracle appears to have been in the speech of the disciples rather than in the hearing of the multitude.

What was the relation of the Lord's promise that His followers were to be baptized with the Holy Spirit (1:5) to the statement, "they were all filled with the Holy Spirit" (v. 4)? Baptism, whether by water or by Spirit, is a kind of attestation. It indicates that a person has been accepted by God or that he stands in some new relationship to God or to His service. Thus the baptism of John with water and the baptizing work of Christ with the Holy Spirit are paralleled six times in the New Testament (Matt. 3:11; Mark 1:8; Luke 3:16; John 1:33; Acts 1:5; 11:16).

The filling with the Spirit, on the other hand, is related to a spoken witness or to an inspired utterance. This term (*pimplēmi*) is almost exclusively a Lukan term in the New Testament, occurring twelve times in Luke and nine in Acts.[14] The accounts about Elizabeth (Luke 1:41), Zacharias (Luke 1:67), Peter (Acts 4:8), the disciples (Acts 4:31), and Paul (Acts 13:9) all illustrate this definition.

Thus, to summarize, we may choose two descriptive words: the baptism relates to *position*; the filling relates to *expression*. In this sense, every Christian has been baptized with the Holy

13. God may and does communicate His message through things familiar to us, but which in mystical experiences take on new significance. (Thus various writers suggest that the "tongues as of fire" might have been caused by rays of sunlight shining through the colonnade of the temple and resting upon the heads of the disciples.) So the use of "as of" is "not to deny the reality of the appearance but to warn the reader that the natural object named does not give an exact description. Fire about the head occurs in both Gentile and Jewish thought as a mark of supernatural favour." K. Lake and H. J. Cadbury, *The Beginnings of Christianity* (London: Macmillan, 1933), IV, 17.

14. Only Matthew 22:10 and 27:48 include the word outside of Luke and Acts.

Spirit, but not every Christian has been filled with the Holy
Spirit. Paul simply affirmed baptism (I Cor. 12:13), but he prayed
for and exhorted believers to be filled with the Spirit (Eph. 3:16;
5:18; 6:10). The latter occurs when the person fulfils God's conditions, even as the disciples obeyed Jesus' command (Luke
24:49).[15]

To avoid the impression that being filled is quantitative (as
one would fill a receptacle with liquid), we need to understand
that the word relates to control or energy. Rather than being
controlled by or energized by fleshly desires or powers, the believers in Jerusalem were endued with divine power. Where
once they were unable to speak—or even to live—except in fear
and selfishness, now they experienced a new energy which gave
them confidence, a concern to witness to their fellows, and a
sense of unity and unselfishness such as they had not known
before.

Finally, the use of *glossolalia* ("tongue-speaking") must be
tested by its content and effects, for it is a common phenomenon
in many religious cultures.[16]

In the New Testament a number of questions are asked about
speaking in tongues: Does it glorify God (Acts 2:11)? Does it
edify believers (I Cor. 14:4–5, 26)? Does it confess Jesus as Lord
(I Cor. 12:3) and as man (I John 4:1–3)? Does it result in one
accepting Jesus Christ as Savior, or becoming a stronger Christian (Acts 2:41)?

b. The reaction of the audience (2:5–13)

Vv. 5–7. Possibly due to the festival season, pilgrims, coming
from various sections of the Roman Empire and beyond, had

15. This is only to recognize the interplay of the divine command and the
human response. God's promises are fulfilled upon the believer's response. "The
Holy Spirit dwelling in us, is one thing; I think this is clearly brought out in
Scripture; and the Holy Spirit upon us for service, is another thing. . . . Before
we pray that God would fill us, I believe we ought to pray Him to empty us,"
wrote D. L. Moody, *Secret Power* (Chicago: The Bible Institute Colportage As-
sociation, n.d.), pp. 33–34.

16. John T. Bunn, "Glossolalia in Historical Perspective," in Watson E. Mills,
ed., *Speaking in Tongues: Let's Talk About It* (Waco, TX: Word Books, 1973),
pp. 36–47.

assembled in Jerusalem. Luke's descriptive term "devout" is used only of Jews in the New Testament (Luke 2:25; Acts 8:2; 22:12).[17]

The hearers were at first "bewildered" ("confounded," KJV) by the speech of the disciples, not because they could not understand, but precisely because they could! It was amazing to hear a group of Galileans (who were noted for their peculiar dialect) speaking in various other dialects.[18]

Vv. 8–11. The list of names is geographical rather than linguistic. Luke listed a good sampling of countries where Jews lived (mainly in the Dispersion). Included in the group were proselytes (Gentiles converted to Judaism).

Generally speaking, the countries are listed in geographical order, from east to west, beginning with three countries beyond the bounds of the Roman Empire (Parthia, Media, and Elam). The last two (Crete and Arabia) seem to be added on.

It is nearly unavoidable to see a parallel with Genesis 10–11, where the list of nations is given together with the confusion of tongues at Babel. Here the names of countries are joined with the restoration of language.

Vv. 12–13. Luke said "amazement and great perplexity" continued (see v. 7). As Robertson says, the people were "wholly at a loss." Some questioned, "What does this mean?" Others mocked, "These men are full of new wine" (KJV). Only here in the New Testament does the word *gleukos* occur; it referred to wine which was still fermenting. The Scriptures frequently contrast drunkenness or madness with some manifestation of the Holy Spirit (Luke 1:15; I Cor. 14:23; Eph. 5:18; cf. I Sam. 1:9–15).

17. *Eulabēs* means "careful, fearing" (in a reverent sense); by extension, "devout or pious." This word is used in the New Testament only of religious attitudes. A closely related word, *eusebēs* ("godly, devout, pious") is used to describe Cornelius (Acts 10:2, 7) and Lot or others like him (II Peter 2:7–9).

18. "The Galilean dialect is specially mentioned as having an indistinct pronounciation of the gutturals (which was, and still is, characteristic of the Samaritans), and also as a dialect in which syllables were often swallowed in such a way that the meaning of words and phrases often became doubtful to a southern Jew." A. Neubauer, "The Dialects of Palestine in the Time of Christ," in *Studia Biblica*, (1885), p. 51, cited by Bruce, *Acts of the Apostles*, p. 84. A. T. Robertson, *Word Pictures in the New Testament* (New York: Richard R. Smith, 1930), III, 23, remarks: "They were not strong on language and yet these are the very people who now show such remarkable linguistic powers."

c. *Peter's speech (2:14–36)*

As was noted previously, Peter's remarks were directed toward explaining the unusual events of the day (by reference to the words of Joel 2:28–32), and toward evangelizing (telling the good news about Jesus) the multitude.

From the structure of Peter's words, notice the following points. The first division (vv. 14–21) relates to prophecy and the coming of the Holy Spirit; the second (vv. 22–28) to prophecy and the death and resurrection of Christ; and the third (vv. 29–36) to the resurrection and ascension of Christ. Peter's conclusion was that Jesus is both Lord and Messiah.

Vv. 14–16. As spokesman for the disciples, Peter began to explain the events which had transpired before the eyes and ears of the people. To begin with, the disciples were not drunk. Simply Peter stated it was only the middle of the morning (reckoning the third hour from sunrise), and the Jews do not take food until the fourth hour. Rather, the explanation is found in the words of the prophet Joel. "This is that" seems to mean what it says, although it does not require that all things included in the prophecy happen at once. Obviously they did not.

Vv. 17–21. John the Baptist (Matt. 3:2) and Jesus (Matt. 4:17) had both declared, "the kingdom of heaven is at hand." With the appearance of the Savior the kingdom had drawn near to men. Following the ascension of our Lord, Peter announced the onset of "the last days" (notice Joel 2:28 simply states "after this"), an expression referring to the onset of the messianic age, the days of the Messiah.[19] Thus the incarnation signaled the first advent of Messiah; the ascension signaled the beginning of a period to be climaxed by the second advent of Messiah.[20]

In verses 17–18, Peter said the Spirit is to be poured out; verses 19–20 refer to signs of judgment in evidence; and in verse 21, salvation (or, deliverance) is promised for all who call on the name of the Lord. Some scholars regard the term "all man-

19. A. Cohen, *The Twelve Prophets* (London: The Soncino Press, 1966), p. 72. See also Isaiah 2:2; Micah 4:1.

20. Homer Hailey, *A Commentary on the Minor Prophets* (Grand Rapids: Baker, 1972), p. 54.

kind" to mean Israel only; the heathen will be destroyed.[21] Others, and rightly so, see people of all nations blessed by this divine visitation.[22] Further, no class distinctions are maintained—sons, daughters, young men, old men, bondslaves (both men and women) all are included.

If we understand the prophecy to include the present age, do we not see many evidences of the Spirit's work in our own day? Is not the Lord once more visiting mankind with outpourings of His Spirit, with portents of judgment, and with deliverance for all who call upon His name? While there will be a great intensity of all these signs in "the great and glorious day of the Lord," as Scripture often indicates,[23] the present days are full of His work in the earth.[24]

Vv. 22–24. Then Peter came to what he really wanted to talk about, that is, the career of our Lord. Peter said a number of things about Jesus in this very short statement. Notice this statement is typical of apostolic preaching. In fact, this outline for Peter's message, one will find, will fit most of the sermons that the apostles delivered to Jewish audiences. These sermons, as recorded in Acts, have some kind of historical introduction or background introduction from the Old Testament. The apostles talked about the Lord, using illustrations from the Old Testament. Peter briefly mentioned Jesus' public ministry (v. 22). The reference to His death was also brief, although important (v. 23). The real point that Peter wanted to make was about the res-

---

21. G. A. Smith, *The Book of the Twelve Prophets* (London: Hodder and Stoughton, n.d.), II, 428.

22. Cohen, *The Twelve Prophets*, p. 72; Hailey, *Minor Prophets*, pp. 53, 54.

23. Notice especially the message of the Apocalypse, and other related passages of Scripture in both Old and New Testaments (e.g., Matt. 24–25; II Thess. 1:5—2:12).

24. Among many recent books, the following give generally sober assessments of the present scene: Erling Jorstad, ed., *The Holy Spirit in Today's Church: A Handbook of the New Pentecostalism* (Nashville: Abingdon, 1973); Frank Stagg, *The Holy Spirit Today* (Nashville: Broadman, 1974); Maynard James, *I Believe in the Holy Ghost* (Minneapolis: Bethany, 1965); K. Dyer, *The Wineskins Are Bursting* (Prospect Heights, IL: Missionary Enterprises, n.d.); W. G. Hathaway, *A Consideration of Modern Pentecostal Phenomena* (Croydon: Heath Press, 1967); J. Elmo Agrimson, ed., *Gifts of the Spirit and the Body of Christ: Perspectives on the Charismatic Movement* (Minneapolis: Augsburg, 1974).

urrection. And on that Peter concentrated. This is exactly the
same pattern as in the parallel sermon in Acts 13, when Paul
spoke to the Jews in the synagogue at Pisidian Antioch. Notice
Paul gave background from the Old Testament, briefly mentioned the Lord's earthly life and death, and then spent a large
part of his message speaking about the resurrected and glorified
Lord. The apostles emphasized the resurrection in their messages because the resurrection is the distinctive element of the
Christian message. There were plenty of messages in those days
of gods who had suffered and died, but there was only one
message that spoke of a resurrected Lord. (I don't mean to elimi-
nate the mythologies in Egypt, such as those relating to Serapis
or others, but these mythologies never asserted that the god truly
returned to life and communion with people on earth, as the
Egyptians themselves would attest.) For this reason the apostles
emphasized the resurrection.

Vv. 25–35. Along with the references to the resurrection, Peter recounted the Old Testament prophecies. This bringing back
to life ("God raised Him up again," v. 24, or, "This Jesus God
raised up again," v. 32) was not accidental. Peter's argument for
these people was, this is what the Old Testament had predicted
would happen. Notice the first argument. David said, speaking
of the Lord Jesus, that God would raise Him up (vv. 25–28).
Again, David, not speaking of himself, said, "The Lord said to
my Lord, Sit at My right hand, Until I make Thine enemies a
footstool for Thy feet" (vv. 34–35).[25] So Peter saw these as Old
Testament predictions of the resurrection of Christ. And these
are important passages because they are used rather frequently
by the apostles.

V. 36. Notice the startling conclusion in verse 36, the last
verse in this section. This is a devastating statement. We have
been too long conditioned by Christian history to really feel the
impact of this statement. If you can, put yourself for a moment
in the place of these people who were listening. First, they were
Jewish people who had long been anticipating the Messiah and
were eagerly looking forward to His coming. Second, their rep-

---

25. See Psalm 16:8–11 and Psalm 110:1. The latter was used by Christ Himself against His opponents (Matt. 22:41–46), and also by the writer to the Hebrews to show the superiority of the Son over the angels (Heb. 1:13).

resentatives had crucified this man, putting Him to death
Roman historians also attest) under the prefect Pontius
He had been crucified for sedition by the Roman government,
as a common criminal, and put into a grave. Peter said, "Therefore let all the house of Israel know for certain that God hath
made Him [and this is the devastating line] both Lord and Christ
[i.e., Messiah]." In effect Peter said, "You killed your own Messiah." Can we imagine the feelings that must have swept over
that group of people as they were faced with this accusation?
Both phrases—"Jesus whom you crucified" and "Christ"—are
significant in this context because Peter again was making use
of Old Testament language and applying it to Jesus. Various Old
Testament passages refer to Jesus as the crucified One, Jesus
regarded as a common criminal, Jesus under the curse of God
because He was hanged on a tree. And this Jesus is the LORD, a
designation that, in the Septuagint, refers to Jehovah of Israel.
Peter said this man Jesus is God from heaven. Also, this man is
the Anointed One, the Messiah, the One whom God has chosen
and sent into the world (Ps. 2). What a contrast between the
crucified criminal and the risen, ascended Lord!

d. Peter's appeal (2:37–41)

When these Jews heard Peter's message, they were "pierced to
the heart" (an alternate rendering is "smitten in conscience").
They said to Peter and the rest of the apostles, "Brethren, what
shall we do?" That is, if what you are saying is really true, what
should we do about it? Peter said, "Repent, and let each of you
be baptized in the name of Jesus Christ for the forgiveness of
your sins; and you shall receive the gift of the Holy Spirit. For
the promise is for you." Notice that—you who have just crucified this man. The promise of the Holy Spirit is for you, if you
will repent. Call upon the name of the Lord. Here is one of the
great allusions to the mercy and forgiveness of God which we
see all through the Old Testament. No matter what the people
of Israel have done, if they come to repentance God will forgive
them.[26]

The phrase "repent and . . . be baptized," sounds very much

26. One of the most beautiful illustrations occurs in the Book of Micah, where
the prophet extols the lovingkindness of the Lord and His faithfulness to His
covenant (7:18–20).

like what we read earlier in the New Testament. In the third and fourth chapters of the Gospel of Matthew or the first chapter of Mark, one will find that this is essentially what John the Baptist cried out, and what our Lord, following him, taught. People were to repent and to receive baptism as a sign of that repentance. That was a rather standard procedure in Jewish life. It does not occasion any great problem to link the two things together, because baptism as John administered it in a public, physical way became a definite confession of people's change of mind (which is what repentance means). Repentance is not something hidden away in one's heart; instead, one is willing to take a public stand and to confess Jesus as the Messiah. That was a hard thing to do under these circumstances, but Peter called for such an expression.

There is a problem of interpretation in verse 38: "Repent, and let each of you be baptized in the name of Jesus Christ for the forgiveness of your sins." Certain of the confessional churches (e.g., the Lutheran church) say that in baptism itself occurs the actual washing away of sins—that when a person is baptized the baptism takes away his sins. On the other hand, from a Baptistic point of view, the baptism is a sign that God had forgiven the sins upon one's repentance. Probably the phrase "for the forgiveness of sins" should be joined not only with baptism but also with repentance: For the forgiveness of sins repent and be baptized. To rephrase this, a person shows true repentance by being baptized, and God has granted forgiveness of his sins.

A further point has been made here by Greek scholar A. T. Robertson regarding the interpretation of that phrase "for the forgiveness of sins." Robertson refers to Matthew 12:41, "The men of Nineveh shall stand up with this generation at the judgment, and shall condemn it because they repented at the preaching of Jonah." The phrase "at the preaching of Jonah" is exactly the same grammatically as the one in Acts 2 which is translated with the word *for*. The preposition represents the Greek word *eis*, translated "at" in Matthew and "for" in Acts. Thus Robertson suggests translating Acts 2:38 as, "Repent and be baptized *because of* the remission of your sins" (italics his), even as men repented "at" or "because of" the preaching of Jonah.

The gift of the Holy Spirit, God's promise to all who call upon Him in repentance and faith,[27] would be bestowed upon these people, said Peter. And thus three thousand people (v. 41) responded to the invitation—an evangelist's dream!

e. Life in the early church (2:42–47)

The new believers immediately shared in the life of the original group—the 120. Notice "they were continually devoting themselves to"—the new way of life was not a hit-and-miss affair.[28]

V. 42. Four elements are indicated. Christian instruction was a primary part of these converts' lives. Even as Jesus had taught His apostles, so now the apostles taught the new converts. Not only the great themes of Jesus' teaching were repeated—the kingdom of God, the death, resurrection, and ascension of Christ, the life devoted to the will of God, and other emphases—but also the teaching was done in the power of and with illumination by the Holy Spirit (see John 14:26; 16:13–15).

Second, fellowship, literally, "a sharing-in-common," was realized. The word may be descriptive of the new way of life (see vv. 44–45), or it may introduce the next two elements, which would be specific examples of fellowship.

Third, the breaking of bread was a sign of the reality of the new family relationship. To break bread was, symbolically, to share one's life with others. It was also a sign of friendship, for to eat at table together was to vow to do one good, not evil. The expression was also used of the Lord's Supper (Acts 20:7).

Fourth, "the prayers" (RSV) indicated the group prayed together, although private prayers would not be ruled out.

Vv. 43–47. The life of the new community was vital. These believers shared their goods (see also 4:32–35), they showed the joy of the new relationship, and they praised God, with the result that numbers were added to the group. Notice the believers bore the witness, and the Lord added the new persons (v. 47).

27. See Galatians 3:14 for a similar word directed to Gentiles, and compare Acts 13:38–39, 52.
28. See also Acts 1:14; 6:4; 12:12; Colossians 4:2.

3. The first apostolic miracle (3)

In chapter 3, the healing of a lame man by Peter became the occasion for another speech, and this is the first recorded miracle by an apostle. Even as in the Gospel narratives, miracles are sometimes occasions for speeches. This is especially so in the fourth Gospel where Jesus' miracles, there called signs, present occasions for some speech or discourse about Himself. See, for example, John 5, in the case of the healing of the paralytic, and John 6, at the feeding of the five thousand. In each case, Jesus made claims for Himself, the speeches growing out of the incident of the sign.

Thus in the Book of Acts the main figures followed much the same pattern: a miracle followed by a speech. This applied mainly to the ministries of Peter and Paul, for no one else was quite so important to Luke. Further, most of the outstanding deeds performed were done by each of them. If Peter healed a lame man, so did Paul (chap. 14); if Peter made an important speech to a Jewish audience (chap. 2) so did Paul (chap. 13); if Peter spoke to a non-Jewish group (chap. 10), so did Paul (17:22–21). These, and a number of other parallels, are a notable feature of Luke's description of the two main figures in his story of early Christianity.

The present narrative has two basic parts—the miracle (vv. 1–10), and the speech explaining it (vv. 11–26)—giving both a visual and oral presentation.

a. Peter healed a lame man at the temple (3:1–10)

Vv. 1–3. According to the Book of Acts there was no sharp change in the behavior of the apostles from their habits before the day of Pentecost. Peter and John, as naturally as could be, went up to the temple at the ninth hour (3:00 P.M.) to pray. This was one of the three hours of prayer in the Jewish day (cf. Dan. 6:10). The apostles continued to frequent the temple in Jerusalem, and to observe the regular hours of prayer. (Notice also this principle in Paul's life, e.g., Acts 21:26; 22:17.) Yet, because the apostles had come to accept Jesus as the Messiah, the temple and the prayers took on new significance. But gradually the breach began to widen between Judaism and Christianity, until the death (in A.D. 62) of James, the leader of the church in Jerusalem; finally, the destruction (in A.D. 70) of the temple by the Romans brought such practices to an end.

In the history of Israel there were two or possibly three temples. The first, and in one sense the greatest, was built by Solomon, and stood for about 350 years, being destroyed by the Babylonians in 586 B.C. The second was built by Zerubbabel following the exile, being completed in 515 B.C. It was often attacked, possibly even ruined. But the third temple was the most extensive of all. Built between 19 B.C. and A.D. 62 (Herod the Great, the most noted architect of Palestine, started this project), it was the sanctuary known to our Lord and the people of the first century. Herod also built many beautiful forums and government buildings, some of them being named in honor of the Caesar. After Herod's death in 4 B.C., construction continued for more than sixty years, and had hardly been completed before the Romans attacked and destroyed the temple in A.D. 70.

The temple area consisted of about thirty-five acres. Irregular in shape, it was about 1020 feet on the north side, 1595 feet on the west, 921 feet on the south, and 1562 feet on the east.[29] Within its outer wall, parts of which still are visible today, was a large courtyard, the court of the Gentiles, an area allowed to non-Jews who came to view the edifice. On a wall 4.5 feet in height were placarded warnings, which said in effect: "Any non-Jew who passes this wall has himself to blame for his death, which will almost surely ensue." If a Gentile entered within that wall, thus defiling the holy buildings, the Jews could put him to death, as the Roman government had granted them that right.

The eastern side of the court was known as Solomon's portico (cf. John 10:23). Possibly the gate into the temple proper, from this east side, was the so-called Beautiful Gate (v. 2).

A flight of fourteen steps led in from this protective wall to the gate, and at the top was a wall forty feet high—a fortification, indeed. At this point the Roman soldiers met the defenders in the great war of A.D. 66–70, when the temple was attacked, looted, and destroyed.

Within this gate was the court of the women; a flight of fifteen

29. Meir Ben-Dov, "Temple of Herod," *The Interpreter's Dictionary of the Bible*, supplementary volume, (Nashville, Abingdon, 1976), p. 870.

steps led up to the court of Israel (where the males of Israel worshiped). At the top of that flight of steps was a gate made of Corinthian bronze, seventy-five feet high and nearly as wide. It required about twenty men, we are told, to open and close it each day.

Beyond the court of Israel stood the altar of sacrifice, the area in which the priests of Israel ministered, and then the sanctuary itself. Here stood a massive porch, 172 feet high and 120 feet wide—Herod's idea of great architecture—and the famous golden vine (some 6 feet long), a symbol of the nation of Israel. (From this vine Jesus may have drawn His illustration of the true vine; see John 15.)

The sanctuary contained the holy place and the holy of holies, the latter being the place of the manifested presence of God; at least it was during the days of Solomon's temple. Around the sanctuary were clustered many other buildings (cf. Mark 13:1). Herein were rooms used for various purposes, such as the meetings of the Sanhedrin (the supreme court of Judaism), lodging for the priests, and storage. The structure was one of the most magnificent of the age; Herod never did anything on a small scale.[30]

Vv. 4–10. Notice the conversation between Peter and John and the lame man, who sat begging at the gate. Peter called to the lame man to look at them, and addressed him pointedly. We hear Peter's words, reminiscent of Jesus' miracle-working in the narratives of the Gospels: "I do not possess silver and gold, but what I do have I give to you: In the name of Jesus Christ the Nazarene—walk" (or, possibly, "rise and walk"). Recall the scene in Luke 5:23. Jesus was confronted by a man brought to Him on a stretcher. As the man wanted to be healed, Jesus said to the people who were listening, "Which is easier, to say, 'Your sins have been forgiven you,' or to say, 'Rise and walk'?" At this the man arose at once, and went to his home glorifying God, and the people were filled with astonishment and began glorifying God.

Observe the close parallel between these two incidents. Jesus

30. For an informative account, see N. H. Snaith, *The Jews from Cyrus to Herod* (Nashville: Abingdon, 1956), pp. 182–190.

healed a man with a command, pointed the man to Himself, healed him, and sent him home rejoicing. Peter healed a man (using a similar command) in the name of the Lord, the man began to praise God, and the people responded in amazement.

b. Peter explained the miracle (3:11–26)

Peter spoke to the people, dwelling on the connection between Jesus and the healing of the lame man (vv. 12–18). Then he appealed to the people to repent, and return to the Lord, language here (vv. 19–26) similar to that in 2:38. Peter wanted to explain to these people who Jesus is, and bring his hearers to acknowledge Him as their Messiah.

In this passage at least six titles are applied to Jesus, which was Peter's way of explaining who He really is.

V. 13. First, Jesus is referred to as God's "Servant" (the same title is repeated in v. 26). Possibly it is significant that Peter's speech began and ended with that title, one reason being that it was a difficult concept for the Jewish people to grasp. Many Jews could not relate this idea of the Servant of Jehovah (common in the Old Testament) to the concept of messiahship. They tended to separate the two. In the Book of Isaiah (see chaps. 42, 44, 49, 50, 52, and 53) the title *Servant* (of the Lord) sometimes refers to the nation of Israel, sometimes to the prophet himself, but at other times appears to refer to the Messiah.

The important point here is that Peter narrowed the meaning of the title, focusing his remarks as if to say, "While 'the Servant' may sometimes refer to the nation of Israel, or to the prophet himself, primarily it refers to Jesus."[31]

V. 14. Second, Peter referred to Jesus as "the Holy and Righteous One." Once again the language is taken from the Old Testament. This is a positive description of our Lord's character, and His standing before God as well. Jesus, Peter affirmed, is holy and righteous before God, and holy and righteous in Himself. (The two are, obviously, closely related.)[32]

---

31. Notice Paul's play on words in Galatians 3:16 when he used the word *seed*. Not "seeds," plural, but "seed," singular, that is, not the nation Israel, but the person Jesus.

32. In the New Testament see further Luke 4:34; 23:47; Acts 4:27, 30; 7:52; 22:14.

Now Peter focused on a contrast: the Holy and Righteous
One versus a murderer (namely, the brigand Barabbas), both of
whom had been presented to the people by Pontius Pilate. Notice the play on words. The name *Bar-abbas* means "son of the
father." Is that not what Jesus had claimed for Himself (cf. Mark
14:62)? Was Barabbas thus a messianic pretender? Did he come
into Jerusalem to be hailed as "Son of the Father"? In the end,
the people chose the murderer and gave Jesus over to death.
That was the choice of the people, but Peter described Jesus, the
true "Son of the Father," as "the Holy and Righteous One."

Vv. 15–16. Third, the title "the Prince of life" once more sets
up a contrast in language. Peter accused his hearers of putting
to death the prince of life. Is it conceivable to do to death one
who possesses life?

At three other places in the New Testament the word translated "prince" occurs.[33] It is the Greek word *archēgos*, a word
used in the Old Testament to describe a leader or a captain (Num.
14:4), or the head of a family or tribe (Num. 13:2), and also as
a leader or originator (cf. LXX, I Macc. 10:47). In Acts 5:31 Peter
referred to Jesus as "a Prince and a Savior." Twice the writer of
Hebrews used it: "the author of their salvation" (2:10), and "the
author . . . of faith" (12:2).

Thus, there are two important meanings to the word, both in
the Old Testament and the New Testament. Sometimes the word
describes a leader, an author, or the source of something, while
in other instances it means a pioneer, one who opens up or
blazes a trail. In His exalted state, Jesus is called a prince; and
in His work of salvation He is called an author or source, for He
opens up the way of salvation to all who call upon His name.
It was faith in Jesus' name that brought new life to the lame
man.

Vv. 17–18. Fourth, in these verses we find one of the most
significant titles in the narrative, indeed, in the entire book:
"Christ." God, declared Peter, announced beforehand by the

33. The Greek word *archēgos* in each case. In Acts 3:15 it is translated as
"source"; in Acts 5:31, as "Prince"; and in Hebrews 2:10 and 12:2, as "author."
See F. F. Bruce, *The Book of Acts*, New International Commentary on the New
Testament series, (Grand Rapids: Eerdmans, 1954), p. 89.

mouth of all His prophets that His Christ (i.e., Messiah) should suffer. The equivalent Hebrew word (in the Old Testament) is translated "Messiah." Could it be that God's Anointed One should suffer? To make the point clear, Peter identified the Messiah as the one who suffered—the suffering Servant (as described by Isaiah).[34] This seems to be an echo of Jesus' teaching on the same point—"Was it not necessary for the Christ to suffer these things and to enter into His glory?" (Luke 24:26). Later in his life, Peter emphasized the same idea in one of his epistles (see I Peter 1:10–11).

Vv. 19–21. Once again Peter called upon his hearers to repent (cf. 2:38) and to return to the Lord. This combination of the two terms is unusual. These words do occur together in Joel 2:14: "turn and relent" (NASB); "turn back and repent" (NEB); or "turn and repent" (RSV). Peter called for a change of direction in one's life and a change of mind with respect to Jesus. That One who had been delivered up, disowned, and put to death was now to be acknowledged as God's Anointed, the Messiah. In turn, God's response would be twofold: He would cleanse these people from their sins,[35] and He would inaugurate the "times of refreshing"—the messianic age. Again, God's action was linked to the words of the prophets (see also v. 18). His word is sure; it will be fulfilled in His own time.

Vv. 22–24. Fifth, a title implicitly applied to Jesus is that of "Prophet," one like Moses. Moses spoke of another great leader like himself (Deut. 18:15), and in the New Testament Peter, Stephen (Acts 7:37), and the author of Hebrews made much of this parallel. Moses was the first prophet and the founder of the first covenant, while Jesus is the second prophet and the founder of the second covenant (Heb. 8–9).

By definition, the word *prophet* means "a spokesman" or "a mouthpiece," that is, one who speaks for another. Even as Moses had been God's first notable spokesman, so our Lord is the sec-

---

34. See E. J. Young, *My Servants the Prophets* (Grand Rapids: Eerdmans, 1952), pp. 191–192.

35. The Greek word *exaleiphō* means "to wash," "to smear," or "to obliterate." It is used in the New Testament of sins (Acts 3:19); of writing (Col. 2:14); of an entry in a book (Rev. 3:5); and of tears (Rev. 7:17; 21:4).

ond. He is not only the second Adam (I Cor. 15:45); He is also
the second Moses (cf. John 1:17).

Vv. 25–26. Finally, Peter referred to Jesus as the seed of Abraham, citing the promise of God to Abraham (Gen. 12:3; 17:8;
22:18). While the term "seed" would normally be taken to mean
the descendants of Abraham, that is, the Hebrew people, Peter
narrowed it to focus upon one person, namely, Jesus. We read
in the New Testament that Abraham looked for the Messiah as
his seed in the ultimate sense, according to the narrative in the
Gospel of John (8:56). Further, Paul wrote that the gospel had
been preached to Abraham (Gal. 3:8), and that the true seed of
Abraham is Christ (Gal. 3:16).

Notice the sequence appearing here, based upon the stories
in the Old Testament. First, Jesus referred to Abraham seeing
His day (John 8:56). Then, Moses looked forward to the prophet
who would come. Finally, David anticipated his descendant
who would sit upon his throne. All these expectations came into
focus in Christ: the Seed, the Prophet, and the King.

Thus Peter appealed to the people to turn around, be converted, and repent, so that their sins might be wiped away, in
order that times of refreshing might come from the presence of
the Lord. Peter seemed to be saying, "This is all that is needed
on your part for the Lord to bring in the anticipated messianic
age." As people turn back to Him, He will respond. How often
the Old Testament prophets had spoken this message. Peter held
out the offer of God's great blessing to the people, a promise
based upon the written Word of God, and made "yea and Amen"
in the living Word of God.

4. The arrest and release of Peter and John (4:1–31)

On account of the disturbance in the temple area, caused by
the healing of the lame man and their preaching about Jesus'
resurrection, the two apostles were arrested (vv. 1–22), then
returned to their fellows to report what had occurred (vv. 23–31).

a. The arrest (4:1–22)

Vv. 1–3. The apostles were accosted by a group described as
"the priests," meaning those serving in the temple (possibly
those officiating at the evening sacrifice), or perhaps referring

to the temple guard; the "captain of the temple guard," possibly the head of the temple police, in rank second only to the high priest (or a subordinate of the chief captain, for the word *stratēgos* is used for both); and "the Sadducees," members of the nobility in Judaism, many of whom were of priestly families (see also the commentary on v. 6).

This group was "greatly disturbed"—in a state of annoyance or distress—due to the disturbance caused by the apostles in the temple area. (The clamor may have disturbed the worship going on at that time of day.) But, more particularly, the Sadducees were upset by the preaching of the doctrine of resurrection, that of Jesus in particular.

The Sadducees held to the books of Moses, the Torah, as alone authoritative (regarding the rest of the books as secondary); refused to accept the oral traditions (the distinctive mark of the Pharisees); were conservative in politics, championing the Roman rule and maintaining the status quo; and denied the intervention of the supernatural in human life.[36] In practice they were "antinomians,"[37] violaters of the covenant of Israel in their way of life.

The Sadducees saw no reference to the resurrection of the dead in their Scriptures. Thus to them the apostles' preaching was in error. So Peter and John were jailed for the night.

V. 4. In contrast, many of the people hearing the message believed. The group now grew to about five thousand men (plus women).[38] To the people of the vicinity the vitality of the messianic community was evident. There was power to heal both the bodies and spirits of men.

Vv. 5–7. In the morning the Sanhedrin met to hear the apostles. This group was the chief governing body of Judaism, a kind of supreme court of Israel. Made up of seventy members (the "elders" represented by the Sadducees and the "scribes" by the Pharisees), it was headed by the high priest. Annas was "high

36. In the New Testament, see Matthew 22:23; Acts 23:8.

37. This term is applied by J. Klausner in *The Messianic Idea in Israel* (New York: Macmillan, 1955), p. 307.

38. The word *andres* means strictly "males." See also the reference to "five thousand men" at the miracle of the loaves (Luke 9:14), and note Matthew 14:21, "besides women and children" (RSV).

priest emeritus" (to use a modern expression), having held the office from A.D. 6–15. Joseph Caiaphas was the current ruler (A.D. 18–36), the same person who had questioned Jesus and sentenced him to death (Mark 14:61–64). Thus, "all the most powerful opponents of the Christians in Jerusalem are gathered together"[39] to interrogate the apostles.

The question was directed to the accused in terms of the "power" or the "name" behind the apostles' healing of the lame man. It was obvious to the council that these men, in themselves, were not capable of such a deed. Notice the pronoun "you" in verse 7, which may be read "people like you."[40] Further, the council perceived Peter and John to be quite ordinary persons (see v. 13).

Vv. 8–12. The manner of Peter's response—"Peter, filled with the Holy Spirit, said to them"—illustrated the Lord's earlier promise of His help in such situations (see Luke 21:12–15). From the events recorded within the pages of Acts, we learn that the Spirit bestows power for special occasions (see further 4:31; 7:55; 13:9, 52). The same man who had cowered before a servant girl, and denied his Lord (Luke 22:56–60), was bold to respond to the high tribunal.

Peter's words centered on Christ: He has been rejected by men but exalted by God, and in Him alone there is salvation for all mankind. The contrasts are vivid.

$$
\begin{array}{ccc}
& \text{Jesus Christ} & \\
\swarrow & & \searrow \\
\text{you crucified} & & \text{God raised} \\
\downarrow & & \downarrow \\
\text{rejected} & & \text{exalted} \\
\searrow & & \swarrow \\
& \text{the only Name} & \\
& \text{(for salvation)} &
\end{array}
$$

The crucified and risen Christ is the way of both condemnation and salvation. His words are "spirit and are life" (John 6:63), but they also will judge men at the last day (John 12:48).

39. Ernst Haenchen, *The Acts of the Apostles: A Commentary* (Philadelphia: Westminster, 1971), pp. 215–216.

40. Bruce, *The Book of Acts*, p. 99, n. 15.

This was the absolute claim Peter laid before the members of the council.

Vv. 13–17. Quite taken aback by the confidence of the apostles, the leaders began to put the picture together. First, they noticed these men were "uneducated" (lit., "unlettered") and "untrained" (i.e., laymen); in other words, ordinary persons. But, second, the leaders began to remember where they had last seen these men and who they were. According to John's Gospel, Peter and John were the two disciples of Jesus who had followed Him into the palace of Joseph Caiaphas, the high priest, on the night of His arrest (John 18:15–16). They had been with Jesus! They were His disciples! They were "the ringleaders of the sect."[41] The same boldness of speech that the Pharisees and Sadducees had seen in Jesus was manifested in His followers.

At this point the council's dilemma was obvious. What could it do with these men? The miracle was well-known in Jerusalem; thus the council could not deny it. Yet to let the apostles continue to speak about Jesus would risk continued disturbances in the city.

Vv. 18–22. Having considered the alternatives, the council rendered a simple decision: the apostles were forbidden "to speak or teach at all in the name of Jesus." It seems significant that the Sanhedrin made no attempt to argue against or deny the resurrection of Christ. Was that a tactical error? Certainly it is clear that the theme of the risen Lord was the paramount emphasis as the apostolic preaching spread out from this point.

In the same manner, the response by the apostles was simple and clear. They must heed God rather than men, and would keep on witnessing about the things they had seen and heard. There may be an echo here of the words of the Hebrew youths arraigned before Nebuchadnezzar (see Dan. 3:16–18), another situation where threat had been made upon the lives of devout people. So also Socrates had replied to his persecutors, "I shall obey God rather than you."[42]

41. This is the expression used by Rackham, *Acts of the Apostles*, p. 59.
42. Plato, *Apology* from *The Dialogues of Plato*, trans. Benjamin Jowett, in *Great Books of the Western World*, vol. 7 (Chicago: Encyclopaedia Britannica, Inc., 1952), p. 206, sec. 29.

At this the council dismissed Peter and John, for public sentiment, at this point, was running in favor of the apostles (v. 21; cf. 2:47).

This raises the interesting point of the loyalty of followers of Jesus. Shall loyalty be to God or to men? The New Testament provides some helpful instruction: "Let every person be in subjection to the governing authorities" (Rom. 13:1); "be subject to rulers, to authorities" (Titus 3:1); and Peter added, "Submit yourself for the Lord's sake to every human institution" (I Peter 2:13). The point at issue appears to be the question of loyalty to God, first and foremost. As far as the human authority does not contravene that, the believer is bound to be an obedient citizen. But when the establishment has stepped in between God and His people, the person must keep his priorities straight.

b. The release and new boldness (4:23–31)

V. 23. Having been released (see v. 21), Peter and John came to the company of believers, who surely must have been praying for them (12:5). The apostles reported all that had transpired.

Vv. 24–28. The prayer of the group consisted first in acknowledging God as Creator of the heaven and the earth. That majestic address is drawn from many Old Testament passages. This was followed by the appeal to the words of Psalm 2, descriptive of the rulers of earth raging against the Lord and His Messiah (see Ps. 2:1–2). This the council had done in rejecting and crucifying Jesus. That had been no coincidence or accident. It was a part of God's predestined plan (2:23).

Vv. 29–31. Even as Peter and John had been bold before the council, now they prayed for boldness to speak the Word of God. Their request was not for cessation of warfare but for courage in witnessing.

To this was added the request for God to confirm the apostles' witness by healings, signs, and wonders. The healing of the lame man had begun this whole episode (3:6–10; 4:22). Further, signs and wonders (2:43; 5:12; 6:8; 7:36; 15:12) were considered "the signs of a true apostle" (II Cor. 12:12).

Once more the emphasis upon the divine response is indicated. The place was shaken and the disciples were filled afresh with the Holy Spirit. As a result, they began to "speak the word of God with boldness"!

The New Testament urges continual fillings with the Spirit (cf. Eph. 5:18, lit., "be being filled"). That is necessary to bold proclamation. And the fillings come in response to prayer and in the face of our need. God meets one at his point of need, and gives as the occasion demands new power. Notice that pattern in the life of our Lord: "while He was praying . . . the Holy Spirit descended upon Him"; "full of the Holy Spirit . . . [He] was led about by the Spirit in the wilderness"; "Jesus returned to Galilee in the power of the Spirit"; and He read from the Book of Isaiah, "The Spirit of the Lord is upon Me" (Luke 3:21–22; 4:1, 14, 18).

5. The community of goods (4:32—5:11)

A more extended description now is given of the community life of the early disciples (see 2:42–47), followed by two particular examples, one involving Barnabas (4:36–37) and another concerning Ananias and Sapphira (5:1–11).

a. The character of the community (4:32–35)

V. 32. The "congregation" (plēthos) is a word used frequently in Acts (see also 6:2, 5; 15:12, 30; and 21:22 in some manuscripts) to refer to the whole body of Christians, and thus is similar to the word (ekklēsia) translated "church" or "assembly."[43] The group was "of one heart and soul," that is, living in a state of unity. Even as the Israelites were instructed to love the Lord and obey Him "with all their heart and soul,"[44] so it was here. The believers' common loyalty to Christ and the filling with the Holy Spirit had fused them together as one.

V. 33. The apostles maintained a dynamic witness to the risen Lord and Messiah, and God enabled them all to carry on this new way of life.

Vv. 34–35. Needy people among the believers were helped by the proceeds from the sale of real estate owned by others in the group. A common fund was set up, with the apostles ad-

43. Plēthos also refers to the body of the Jews (Acts 19:9; 25:24). See the interesting use of the word in 28:3, a "bundle" of sticks. There is a definitive discussion of the term in Lake and Cadbury, Beginnings, IV, 47–48.

44. Deuteronomy 6:5; 10:12; 11:13; 13:3; 26:16; 30:2, 6, 10.

ministering the freewill offerings. Later, as we shall see (6:1–6), this ministry was delegated to others.

While for the moment the wealthier members were able to help by their contributions, soon their resources were drained, and the church in Jerusalem came into a chronic state of poverty. (See Acts 11:27–30; 24:17; Rom. 15:25–26; I Cor. 16:1–3; II Cor. 8–9; Gal. 2:10.)

  b. *The case of Barnabas (4:36–37)*
The first of Luke's two examples is a positive one. Barnabas is named as a contributor to the common fund. At least four things are said of him: his character—he was nicknamed "the son of encouragement"[45] by the apostles, and nearly everywhere Barnabas appeared he was engaged in helping people (9:27; 11:27–30; 15:35–36); his family background—he was a Levite, a Jew of the priestly tribe; his birthplace—he was a Jew of Cyprus (thus a Hellenistic Jew), speaking the Greek language; and his economic status—he was a landowner, sufficiently well-to-do to sell some property to aid the poor of the congregation.

  c. *The case of Ananias and Sapphira (5:1–11)*
A negative example was also recorded by Luke. This was the first inkling of outward sin in the nascent church.

Vv. 1–2. The man and his wife owned property, sold it, and brought the money to the apostles (as 4:34–35 has indicated). Yet they were deceitful in their seeming act of compassion. They agreed to give (as if giving the whole amount of the sale), yet "kept back" some of the price for themselves. The same word (*enosphisato*) occurs in Joshua 7:1, where Achan "acted unfaithfully" (NASB) or "committed a trespass" (KJV), and Titus 2:10, where "pilfering" (NASB) or "purloining" (KJV) is warned against.

Vv. 3–6. Peter made two assertions. He charged Ananias with lying to the Holy Spirit; not simply to men, but to God. The presence of the Holy Spirit, not only in Peter but also within the community, makes this quite understandable. Second, Peter affirmed that all giving was to be regarded as voluntary, and that private ownership of one's property was retained.

---

45. The etymology of the name is difficult. Along with the lexicons and dictionaries, see Lake and Cadbury, *Beginnings*, IV, 49; Bruce, *The Book of Acts*, p. 109; Haenchen, *Acts of the Apostles*, pp. 231–232.

The passage is an important indication of both the personality and the deity of the Holy Spirit. To say He was present was to say God was present.

Immediately upon hearing Peter's pronouncement of judgment, Ananias "fell down and breathed his last"—we might say he collapsed and expired. This was not simply the result of a shock. Ananias was struck down by divine judgment. It was indeed "the day of visitation" (cf. I Peter 2:12) for Ananias.

Vv. 7–11. Then entered Sapphira. Peter virtually repeated the examination, confronted her with the accusation, and pronounced judgment. Their complicity had been unmasked, and she, too, fell down and died.

Both in verses 5 and 11 the result of the incidents is noted: "great fear" fell upon those knowing of the judgment. The church[46] was faced with the reality of the holiness of God—"Let every one who names the name of the Lord abstain from wickedness" (I Tim. 2:19).

6. The arrest of all of the apostles (5:12–42)

Following the incidents in 4:32—5:11, the main narrative continues. The apostles continued their ministry (vv. 12–16), were jailed, interrogated, and threatened (vv. 17–32), and were released upon the advice of Gamaliel (vv. 33–42).

a. The ministry of the apostles (5:12–16)

V. 12. The mention of "signs and wonders" continues the thought from 4:30, and the reference to "one accord"[47] continues the emphasis of unity begun in 1:14 ("with one mind"). It was not Peter alone, but all the apostles who were involved in the ministry.

V. 13. People kept their distance from the group due to the events that had been occurring. It was not due to opposition, for

---

46. This is the first occurrence of the word "church" (ekklēsia) in the text of Acts, except in the Western (D) text, where it appears in 2:47 (and so in KJV). The term referred to an official assembly of the citizens of a Greek city to conduct their business; the "congregation" of Israel in the wilderness (Acts 7:38); and the body of believers in Jerusalem (and later, in various locations throughout the empire), as well as the whole body (cf. Acts 5:11 with Eph. 1:22–23).

47. See footnote 6.

the people "held them in high esteem," but due to the awe produced by the spiritual power among the believers.

Vv. 14–16. Rather than being diminished in size by the awe-inspiring events, the community grew as many believers were added—"multitudes (*plēthē*) of men and women." Miracles of healing took place through the apostles; even Peter's shadow passing over the sick was efficacious (just as virtue had gone out through touching Jesus' garments—see Luke 8:43–44).[48] Luke emphasized "they were all being healed" (cf. Mark 6:56).

b. The apostles jailed again (5:17–32)

Vv. 17–18. Once more the Sadducees, namely, the high priest and his colleagues, appear. A new motive for their opposition is mentioned—this time, jealousy. Describing a characteristic of the Jewish leaders (whether Sadducees or Pharisees), Paul said of them, ". . . they have a zeal for God, but not in accordance with knowledge" (Rom. 10:2).[49] Possibly they recalled their earlier frustrations during Jesus' ministry, when they feared the "many signs" would bring about unrest and, possibly, new revolutionary movements (see John 11:47–53). Thus the Sadducees jailed the apostles once more.

Vv. 19–20. An angel of the Lord came to the apostles, opened the gate, brought them out, and ordered them to go and continue to "speak to the people." This was the very thing the apostles had been ordered to cease doing by the council at the first arrest (4:17).

Four times in Acts an angel of the Lord appeared to carry out a divine command: to release the apostles from jail (5:19); to guide Philip in his preaching (8:26); to release Peter from prison (12:7–9); to smite Herod Agrippa I (12:23).[50] The term "angel of the Lord" refers to a messenger, God's appointed servant. Due to the variety of usage, one cannot always be certain of the form of the angel. At times it was a heavenly being; at others a human

---

48. See also the case of the handkerchiefs or aprons touched by Paul which brought healing to the afflicted (Acts 19:11–12).

49. See also Acts 13:45, where the Jews in Antioch (Pisidia) were "filled with jealousy" over the response of the people to the preaching of Paul and Barnabas.

50. Rackham, *Acts of the Apostles*, pp. 71–72, has a lengthy comment about the idea of "the angel of the Lord" in the Scriptures.

being; at others a way of describing God's own action. Later in Acts, Peter was released from prison under very similar circumstances, and that account is more detailed (12:7–9).

Vv. 21–25. The Sanhedrin was much perplexed upon discovering the escape of the prisoners, for the report was brought to the council, "Behold, the men whom you put in prison are standing in the temple and teaching the people" (v. 25). Amazingly, the guards were still at the doors of the jail and no one had seen the apostles leave. The members of the Sanhedrin wondered what would happen next!

Vv. 26–28. Rather gingerly the apostles were accosted by the temple guards and returned to the council. There was no force or violence used, for the people were definitely on the side of the apostles.

No mention was made of the arrest or the escape; the high priest simply put to the apostles the question of their disobedience to the orders of the council (4:18). Caiaphas referred to Jesus as "this man" (v. 28), a practice considered by some scholars to show Jewish reluctance to pronounce the name *Jesus*.

Vv. 29–31. Peter's answer to the question was a firm statement of conscience. Obedience to God must, under such circumstances, be preferred above obedience to men. That was, of course, a well-known principle in Jewish history, and the idea of obedience or subjection is frequent in Peter's own writing (see I Peter 1:2, 14, 22; 3:1, 6; 4:17).[51]

One Greek text of Acts puts the statement in an interesting form: "And Peter answered and said to him, Whom is it right to obey, God or men? and he said, God."[52] It was here, of course, a question as to who best represented the mind of God—Peter or Caiaphas.

Again the message concerning Jesus was proclaimed and the offer of repentance and forgiveness of sins was declared—a point that is "part and parcel of the kerygma" (cf. 2:38 and 3:19).[53]

---

51. E. F. Harrison, *Acts: The Expanding Church* (Chicago: Moody, 1976), p. 99.

52. See comment in Lake and Cadbury, *Beginnings*, IV, 59, and III, 53.

53. Haenchen, *Acts of the Apostles*, p. 251.

Christ died, He was raised up, and He was exalted to God's right hand!

V. 32. The apostles described themselves once more as "witnesses" (see Luke 24:48; Acts 1:8, for the commission by the risen Lord; and Acts 1:22; 2:32; 3:15). They were witnesses to the events[54] of Jesus' life, death, and resurrection. The Holy Spirit is also a witness to Jesus (John 15:26), and God imparts Him to all "those who obey Him" (i.e., believers in the good news about Jesus).

c. The advice of Gamaliel (5:33–42)

V. 33. Upon hearing Peter's remarks, the Sanhedrin was infuriated. The expression "they were cut to the quick" translates dieprionto, literally, "they were sawn through" (cf. I Chron. 20:3).[55] As a result, they desired to kill the apostles. Such a decision would need the consent of the whole court, and the Pharisaic members seemed not to be of the same mind as the high priest and his Sadducean cohorts.

V. 34. The Pharisee Gamaliel intervened and gave orders for the accused to be put outside the council chamber while the group discussed their case. Rabban Gamaliel was the first of a line of distinguished teachers to bear the honored title (as distinct from the more ordinary "Rabbi"). He was the leader of the school of Hillel, and, according to Acts 22:3, was the teacher of Saul of Tarsus. His eminence is epitomized in the statement later written in the Mishnah: "Since Rabban Gamaliel the Elder died there has been no more reverence for the Law, and purity and abstinence died out at the same time."[56]

Vv. 35–37. Gamaliel's advice was, first of all, a word of caution against rash—and irremediable—action. He illustrated this point with descriptions of two historical incidents. The first concerned an insurgent named Theudas, who was executed for his

---

54. The term here translated "things" is the word rhēmatōn, usually translated "words" or "utterances" (see Acts 5:20, RSV), but compare Acts 10:37, "thing" or "event."

55. Recall the term katenygēsan in Acts 2:37—"they were pierced to the heart." There the response was very different from that of the Sanhedrin in 5:33.

56. Sotah 9.15 (Danby).

attempt to seize leadership from the existing government.[57] The second, not quite so effective an example, was the case of the reputed founder of the militant zealot movement, Judas of Galilee, who raised a cry against the Roman census of A.D. 6. While he was killed by the Romans, his followers carried on—as an underground movement—and caused trouble, eventuating in the disastrous war of A.D. 66–73 which destroyed the Jewish state.[58]

Vv. 38–39. Gamaliel's advice was, in essence, wait and see. His logic was clear: If the apostles are purely men, their movement will fail; but if they be God's men, do not take sides against God! People do not always follow this advice; Gamaliel's pupil Saul of Tarsus was of quite a different mind. He fought bitterly against the believers.

V. 40. Curiously enough, while the council took Gamaliel's advice, they flogged the apostles, a kind of punishment under which serious injury, or even death, might result. This punishment consisted of thirty-nine lashes, a penalty set by the Mosaic legislation (Deut. 25:3).[59] Once more the council members warned the prisoners to speak no more in the name of Jesus.

Vv. 41–42. Two things are recorded about the apostles after their release. First, they rejoiced that God had considered them worthy of suffering "for the Name" (NIV; an unusual expression that occurs again in III John 7). Second, they kept on preaching and teaching that Jesus is the Messiah, even as they had done

57. The chronological and historical setting of Theudas' rebellion is a vexing problem. To begin with, the only Theudas known outside the New Testament (in Josephus, *Antiquities* 20. 5.1–2) was a rebel during the procuratorship of Cuspius Fadus (A.D. 44–46), some ten years later than the time of Gamaliel's speech. But if Luke's historical sense is to be trusted, there must have been an earlier Theudas, for he is placed before Judas the Galilean (A.D. 6). On the question see, among others Bruce, *The Book of Acts*, pp. 124–25; Harrison, *Acts*, pp. 101–102; and for a contrary opinion see Haenchen, *Acts of the Apostles*, pp. 252–257; Johannes Munck, *The Acts of the Apostles* (Garden City, NY: Doubleday, 1967), pp. 48, 51.

58. The zealots affirmed that loyalty must be to God alone—for He is King—and to pay taxes to a foreign government was, in effect, treasonous.

59. Actually the limit was forty lashes, but the Jews limited it to one less, in case there would be a miscount and more than forty would be administered, thus bringing guilt upon those who had sentenced the accused.

after the first warning. Thus their lives were characterized by
joy, because of Jesus, and they ministered as His witnesses,
speaking by the power of the Spirit.

B. The Ministry of Stephen (6:1—8:3)

1. The appointment of the Seven (6:1–7)

Even while the growth of the body of believers in Jerusalem
was continuing, a situation began to develop which spelled danger to the community.

V. 1. The word "complaint" translates *goggysmos*, literally,
"a whispering," "a murmuring," or "a smoldering discontent."
While the surface appeared calm and serene, there was trouble
in the church, a problem that could soon surface and cause
serious disruption.

How did the problem arise? There was a conflict between
Hellenists and Hebrews regarding the daily dole of money or of
food (cf. 4:34–35). Who were these people? The term "Hellenistic Jews" seems to derive from a verb referring to the adoption
of the Greek language or customs, while "Hebrews" appears (at
least, in other passages, e.g., Phil. 3:5) to refer to Hebrew na-
tionality or language. Probably the two groups were the Greek-
speaking Jewish Christians and the native Palestinian Jewish
Christians.[60] The language difference itself could have contributed to a sense of discontent and jealousy.

Vv. 2–4. Here alone in Acts the title "the twelve" is used with
reference to the apostles. They took things in hand at once,
called together the congregation, and proposed action.

The proposed solution was a council (dare we say "commit-
tee"?) of the seven to handle the details of care for widows, a
practice later explicitly spelled out for the churches (I Tim.
5:3–16). Some scholars see the influence of a Jewish institution,
because in Jewish communities the local council usually was
made up of seven men called the "Seven of the Town" or "Seven
Best of the Town."[61]

---

60. For scholarly discussions see Lake and Cadbury, *Beginnings*, V, 59–74;
H. Windisch, "*Hellenes* in the N.T.," *TDNT*, II, 508–516.
61. Haenchen, *Acts of the Apostles*, p. 263.

These seven men were to be selected by the congregation and appointed by the apostles. Notice the qualifications: "of good reputation" (lit., "witnessed to," meaning characterized by a good witness); "full of the Spirit" (see v. 5, where it is made clear the Holy Spirit is meant); and full of "wisdom" (persons of sensitivity and practical insight).

Who were these seven, in contrast to the apostles? No title was given to the seven. The "ministry of tables" ("to serve tables," v. 2) is the translation of *diakonein*, from which root we derive our English term *deacon*. Probably Rackham's comment is judicious: "Though neither a presbyterate nor diaconate, they include both offices and are the ancestors of both presbyters and deacons" (see I Tim. 3:1–13).

The apostles would "devote" themselves (see also Acts 1:14; 2:42; cf. 2:46) to prayer, a practice highly valued in Jewish life, and to the "ministry of the word," that is, teaching (see also 2:42; cf. Luke 1:2).

Vv. 5–6. So the congregation selected the Seven. These men all bore Greek names, and the last named, Nicolas, was a proselyte (a Greek convert to Judaism) of Antioch (Syria). Stephen is the only one of whom comment is made—"a man full of faith and of the Holy Spirit"—which was Luke's way of introducing the person who would occupy the center stage (from this point through Acts 8:3). The only other person mentioned again in Acts is Philip the evangelist, whose ministry is described in 8:5–40, and who was Paul's host (21:8–9).

By prayer and imposition of hands the apostles gave official recognition to the Seven. An ancient custom, the laying on of hands signified the transfer of something from one to another.[62] Here laying on of hands was apparently the investure with authority for the new ministry. In later examples, this procedure refers to ordaining people to a new work (Acts 13:3), or conferring the gift of the Holy Spirit (Acts 8:17; 9:17; 19:6). Paul wrote of the imposition of a "spiritual gift" by this means (I Tim. 4:14; II Tim. 1:6).

V. 7. Luke gave another progress report: the spread of the

---

62. See the essay by Silva New in Lake and Cadbury, *Beginnings*, V, especially pp. 137–138.

gospel continued, the number of the disciples increased greatly, and "a great many" of the priests became believers.

Who were the "priests" (the only mention of this in Acts)? Probably not Sadducean priests, due to the number implied. Were they some of the less pretentious temple staff, or Pharisaic priests, or Essenes? The issue is not clarified by Luke.

2. Stephen's defense and death (6:8—8:1a)

a. Stephen's ministry in Jerusalem (6:8-15)

Stephen was "the connecting link between S. Peter and S. Paul—a link indispensable to the chain."[63] One may note that at the beginning of Acts Peter is prominent, and at the latter part Paul occupies most attention. Peter's ministry was primarily to the Jews; Paul's to the Gentiles (cf. Gal. 2:7-8). Stephen represented the transition from one emphasis to another.

V. 8. Stephen's ministry was characterized by his "grace and power" ("faith and power," KJV),[64] both terms referring to the working of the Holy Spirit—Who is both Helper and Dynamic. This issued in "great wonders and signs," a repeated emphasis in Acts (see before this 2:22, 43; 4:30; 5:12; and later 7:36; 8:13; 14:3).

Vv. 9-11. Stephen's opponents were Hellenistic Jews (i.e., Greek-speaking Jews, from territories outside Palestine), and they represented the Synagogue of the Freedmen (some older translations render the title as "Libertines") in Jerusalem.[65] These Jews accosted Stephen, being unable to display the same religious wisdom he evidenced (an example of Jesus' promise in Luke 21:15). Thus they instigated false witnesses against him in order to attempt to stop his preaching. The charge was blasphemy against Moses and against God. In this circumstance, "blasphemy" represents a wider use of the term than actually

---

63. Rackham, Acts of the Apostles, p. 88.

64. Bruce M. Metzger, The Text of the New Testament: Its Transmission, Corruption, and Restoration (New York: Oxford University Press, 1968, 2nd ed.), pp. 221-223, has an illuminating presentation of the evidence on this textual variant.

65. For a discussion of the possible renderings of this passage see Lake and Cadbury, Beginnings, IV, 66-68.

pronouncing the divine name. In fact, the charge was quite similar to that made against Jesus at His trial (cf. Mark 14:57–64).

Vv. 12–15. Dragging Stephen before the council, as had happened to the apostles earlier, the Hellenistic Jews accused Stephen of speaking against the temple and the Law. Thus he was charged with defiling both the national worship of Judaism and the abiding truth and authority of the Law. As given, the words about the temple were traced back to "this Nazarene, Jesus" (cf. John 2:19–21; and see Mark 14:58).

At this point Stephen's face appeared to the Sanhedrin to be "like the face of an angel." This expression may be substituted for "being full of the Spirit" (7:55), for immediately Stephen began to speak (7:2). Rackham writes that "at the thought of the opportunity, his face glowed with enthusiasm also."[66]

b. Stephen's speech before the Sanhedrin (7:1–53)

While often referred to as "Stephen's defence," the speech does not actually have this character. Rather Stephen passionately attacked the attitudes and actions of the Jewish people over the preceding centuries, their attachment to the temple, and their rejection of the prophets. No mention is made of the Law as such.

The speech may be analyzed succinctly under the following divisions: the patriarchal period (vv. 2–16); the Mosaic period (vv. 17–43); the monarchical period (vv. 44–50); and Stephen's accusation (vv. 51–53).

Stephen included in his remarks several references to divine revelations and appearances (vv. 2, 20, 30), and to foreshadowings of the Messiah (vv. 25, 35, 36, 37, 38, 52).

The period of the patriarchs was initiated when "the God of glory appeared" to Abraham (v. 2). The emphasis is upon God's activity in the lives of these people, and their faith and response to Him. God called and delivered them. Nor was His activity confined to any one special place.

The period of Moses, especially including the preparation of Moses as the Israelites' deliverer, and the dramatic events of the exodus from Egypt, was a vivid foreshadowing of the Messiah,

---

66. Rackham, *Acts of the Apostles*, p. 91.

the deliverer of the people of God. God "granted deliverance" (*sōtēria*, lit., "salvation," v. 25); He "sent ... a deliverer" (*lytrōtēs*, lit., "redeemer," v. 35), and Moses "led them out" of bondage (v. 36). Moses also testified of "a prophet" (v. 37) who should come, a word also pointing to Christ (cf. Acts 3:19–23).

The *period of the monarchy*, in Stephen's speech, began with the time of the tabernacle, which led on to the temple ("a dwelling place for the God of Jacob"). God gave directions for building both these centers of worship. The people made the mistake, then, of thinking that God could be, or was, confined to a place. This Stephen pointedly disavowed (v. 48)—rather God is the Creator, and He cannot be restricted by men.

Stephen's accusation was that the Jews were "always resisting the Holy Spirit" (v. 51). So the psalmist (Ps. 106:33) and Isaiah (63:10) had reported, and the Jews of Stephen's day had followed the pattern. Paul had written about quenching the Spirit by despising the words of prophecy (I Thess. 5:19–20).

V. 52. Again, Stephen accused these Jews' fathers of persecuting and killing the prophets, and his hearers of betraying and murdering the Righteous One (a title of Jesus, Acts 3:14; 22:14).[67]

V. 53. Finally, Stephen contended the Jews had not kept the law of God, delivered to them by angels (cf. Gal. 3:19; Heb. 2:2). Even early in their history, after promising that "all that the Lord has spoken we will do" (Exod. 19:8), they broke the commandments, beginning with faithlessness and idolatry (Exod. 32:1–4). The centuries between had shown no decided change for the better!

c. Stephen's death (7:54—8:1a)

V. 54. The reaction of the Sanhedrin was immediate. "They were cut to the quick" (cf. 5:33, concerning the apostles) and "began gnashing their teeth [in rage]" (a common Old Testament expression indicating anger and desire to destroy).[68]

Vv. 55–56. To the martyr was revealed the glory of God and

---

67. The Book of Enoch 38:2 uses this title, as one of several, for the Messiah. In the New Testament, only the speeches in Acts contain the title (but cf. Matt. 27:19; Luke 23:47).

68. See Job 16:9; Psalms 35:16; 37:12; 112:10; Lamentations 2:16.

the sight of Jesus standing at His right hand. Stephen saw "the Son of Man" waiting to welcome Him—the only place in the New Testament the risen Jesus is pictured as standing, for He "sat down" after completing the work of redemption (Heb. 10:12).

This is the only use of the title "the Son of Man" by anyone except our Lord Himself during His earthly stay. And Stephen had grasped the title's tremendous significance. That One rejected by men had been exalted by God and seated on "the throne of the Universe."[69] With this goes the idea that the way to the presence of God is open to all. No restriction can be placed upon it any longer. Such a word, of course, would be disagreeable to the guardians of the sacred temple as they listened to Stephen.

Vv. 57–58. The pronoun "they" is unclear. Was it the Sanhedrin who now vented its anger? Or was it the mob, infuriated, who rushed upon Stephen and lynched him? While certainty is difficult, the presence of the witnesses possibly implies an execution legally carried out. And the lack of time taken to obtain the permission of the Roman prefect of Judea, Pontius Pilate, may imply that it was a case of political expediency. The governor may not have been interested in any further trouble in Judea.[70]

By reference to the witnesses placing their "robes" (himatia, "outer garments") at the feet of "a young man named Saul," Luke introduced his chief character into the book. This scene would never be wiped away from Saul's memory (see Acts 22:20).

Vv. 59–60. As he was being stoned to death,[71] Stephen twice spoke out to the Lord Jesus—first to ask Jesus to receive his spirit (cf. Luke 23:46); then to grant forgiveness to his killers (cf. Luke 23:34). At his death he gave voice once more to the central affirmation of the early church: Jesus is Lord!

Stephen's death is described as "falling asleep." So Luke recorded it of David in a speech by Paul (13:36); and Paul in his

69. The phrase used by W. Manson, *The Epistle to the Hebrews* (London: Hodder & Stoughton, 1951), p. 32.

70. Possibly Pilate had established "a neutral understanding" with the high priest; Bruce, *The Book of Acts*, p. 170.

71. See the directives regarding this method of execution in Deuteronomy 17:6–7; Mishnah, *San.* 6:1–4.

letters used it of believers generally (I Cor. 15:6, 18, 20; I Thess. 4:13, 14, 15).

V. 1a. Luke made clear what Saul's attitude was. Saul was not simply a passive spectator, but one in hearty accord with the action taken against the accused. Was this the spark that ignited the explosion?

3. The onset of persecution (8:1b–3)

This first major section of Acts is concluded with the reason for the scattering of the church out of Jerusalem; it was caused by "a great persecution." Saul of Tarsus took the lead in that persecution.

V. 1b. All except the apostles were scattered throughout Judea and Samaria. Why were the apostles not included? Possibly the Hellenistic leaders (such as Stephen) were the targets of persecution. The Hebrews among the leadership had not seemed to the establishment to be set against the traditions as, for example, Stephen had been. For the time being they were safe (but see 12:1–5). Yet this very means was used to begin the fulfillment of the Lord's commission to the apostles—the witness must go out into "all Judea and Samaria" (Acts 1:8).

Vv. 2–3. While "devout men," presumably from among the Jews of the city, buried Stephen, Saul launched his attack. He "began ravaging" the church, as a wild animal attacks and tears the body of its victim. Much more was to follow, as Acts and Paul's letters testify (e.g., Acts 22:4; 26:10–11; I Cor. 15:9; Gal. 1:13).

Saul parted company with his conciliatory master, Gamaliel. Saul's way would be the way of action, drastic and zealous. He would defend the name of his God and the honor of Judaism to the full extent of his powers. How could these who exalted the name of a crucified imposter be allowed to live? The movement must be exterminated.

III. Transition: Into Judea and Samaria (8:4—11:18)

The persecution scattered the believers to various parts of the area—some to Samaria (8:5–25) and others to more distant parts (11:19). Luke divided his account into two major sections—in the language of 8:4 and 11:19, "then those who were scattered went about"[72]—indicating the summary of the action.

V. 4. Luke's phrase describing the activity of these scattered believers is "preaching the word." The verb is *euaggelizo*, usually meaning "to tell the good news"; here it apparently means "to preach" (cf. the phrase in 4:29 and 11:19, "to speak the word," probably an equivalent).

A. The Ministry of Philip (8:5–40)

At this point one of the Seven (6:5) came into prominence as an evangelist, carrying the message beyond the limits of Jerusalem and Judea. This represented a transition from the Jewish audience (chaps. 1–5) to a Gentile audience (chap. 10, with Peter in Caesarea, and chaps. 11ff., with Barnabas and Saul in Antioch and regions beyond).

1. Philip and the Samaritans (8:5–13)

V. 5. Philip (called "the evangelist" in 21:8) bridged the gap between the Jews and the Samaritans. There had been bad feeling between the two groups for many years. The Jews regarded the Samaritans as half-breeds in race and religion, an attitude stemming from the days of the Assyrian captivity of Israel (the northern kingdom), and the northerners returned the feeling in kind.[73] Like the Jews, the Samaritans had a place of worship (on Mount Gerizim beside Shechem, John 4:20) and looked for Messiah (John 4:25).

72. The phrase *hoi men oun diasparentes dielthon*, used in both 8:4 and 11:19, indicates the beginning of a narrative about the dispersed believers.
73. See, for example, II Chronicles 30:10; and also II Kings 17:33–35.

In Samaria,[74] Philip proclaimed Christ (i.e., the Messiah) to the people. This message was quite in keeping with their expectations.

Vv. 6–8. With one accord the people responded, being aided in their response by the signs which Philip was performing. These attesting miracles consisted of exorcisms, and healing of the paralyzed and lame,[75] and produced "much rejoicing in that city."

Vv. 9–11. Simon Magus (the magician) had for some time before this[76] been amazing the people of Samaria by his magic arts, what Harrison[77] calls "the most degraded form of religion in the Hellenistic age" (see also Acts 13:6; 19:19). People of the class called magi (cf. Matt. 2:1) were numerous and influential. The class was comprised of a variety of occupations. Among them were exorcists, healers, and wonder-workers; astrologers and spiritualists; philosophers and teachers of morality; and prophets, who claimed divine inspiration.

Claiming to be someone great, Simon had apparently convinced many, for people called him "the Great Power of God." Some scholars consider the words "of God" to be a gloss on the text, for Simon was claiming to be "the highest divinity itself,"[78] rather than a kind of pseudo-Messiah. Other scholars call him "the Grand Vizier of the supreme God,"[79] who brought both divine power and divine revelation to men.

V. 12. Here is the first mention in Acts of "the kingdom of God" by the Christian preachers. (See Acts 1:3, where Jesus had instructed His disciples in the things "concerning the kingdom of God," and the disciples' resultant question in 1:6.) In this case the message was directed toward Samaritans; later Luke

---

74. We cannot be certain to what city in Samaria Philip traveled. Was it "the city" (Sebaste, rebuilt by Herod the Great and named in honor of Augustus Caesar)? Or was it "a city" (if so, no certain place was designated, although some favor Gitta, the birthplace of Simon Magus)?

75. Compare Acts 3:2; 9:33; 14:8 for similar miracles.

76. *Prouperchen* means "before then" (see also Luke 23:12).

77. Harrison, *Acts*, p. 137.

78. Haenchen, *Acts of the Apostles*, p. 303.

79. Bruce, *The Book of Acts*, p. 179.

recorded cases involving Jews (19:8; 28:23), Gentiles (28:30–31), and believers (14:22; 20:25).

The concept of the kingdom was rooted in the Hebrew Scriptures, in which God is regarded as the King who shall "reign forever and ever" (Exod. 15:18; Ps. 10:16; 29:10). Ultimately the Lord will be king over all the earth (Zech. 14:9) and every knee shall bow to Him (Isa. 45:23). In Acts the theme is closely related to the proclamation of the name of Jesus Christ (8:12; 28:23, 31). Thus we may conclude Luke regarded the message of the kingdom as that of the good news (the gospel) of God's redemptive plan in Christ.[80] The only clear eschatological reference appears to be in 14:22.

V. 13. At this point we learn "even Simon himself believed." Considered within the context of this verse alone the conversion of Simon may seem genuine enough. Yet there are certain other considerations. First, the words of Peter to Simon (see vv. 20–23) appear to indicate an unsatisfactory state of heart. Second, Simon was a magician, and was doubtless impressed by the miracles and words of Philip. Was Simon's belief, therefore, grounded in those miracles, rather than in the name of the Messiah? Third, a faith grounded in miracles alone is not always genuine, although it may be sincere as far as it goes. John's Gospel, especially, records words of Jesus to this effect (John 2:23–25; 20:29).

2. Peter and John visited Samaria (8:14–25)

At first mention it may seem strange to see these two apostles making their way into Samaria to impart the Holy Spirit to the new believers. Had Jesus not told His disciples, "Do not enter any city of the Samaritans" (Matt. 10:5)? And had not John, with his brother James, wanted "to command fire to come down from heaven and consume them [the Samaritans]" (Luke 9:54)?

Things had changed. When commissioning His disciples just prior to the ascension, Jesus had included Samaria as an area of their witness (Acts 1:8). And the Holy Spirit had brought a change in the apostles' outlook toward others. John became known as "the apostle of love."

80. While we need not identify the church and the kingdom, the relatedness of them seems clear in such a passage as Matthew 16:18–19.

Vv. 14–17. The two apostles were delegated by the church in
Jerusalem to investigate and confirm the reports of Philip's ministry in Samaria. The new converts had not yet received the
Holy Spirit, only baptism in the name of the Lord Jesus, for in
Acts the Spirit was imparted to converts only in the presence
of apostles (see the examples in Acts 2:38–41; 10:44; 19:6). Yet
two further remarks are needed. First, this does not mean the
Spirit is imparted necessarily by the laying on of hands (e.g.,
10:44). Second, the New Testament generally assumes that all
who have believed in Christ have received the gift of the Holy
Spirit (e.g., Rom. 8:9; II Cor. 1:21–22; Gal. 4:4–6; Eph. 1:13–14).

Probably the emphasis here was needed because this was a
group of non-Jewish believers (as was the case in 10:44–48 and
19:1–6). Bringing Samaritans into the church was no less as-
tounding than bringing Gentiles into the church (cf. 11:17–18).
So a special sign was needed at this initial breakthrough.[81]

A further point of import here is the phrase "baptized in [lit.,
into] the name of the Lord Jesus." The words *into the name of*
were common in commercial use, signifying a transfer of property. Thus the believers became the property of the Lord Jesus.
Such language prepares the way for the reader of Paul's letters
where the "in Christ" formula appears so often, or where he
writes of being "baptized into Christ Jesus" (Rom. 6:3; Gal. 3:27).

Vv. 18–19. Amazed at the apostles' power to bestow the Holy
Spirit, Simon offered them money to gain that same authority.
Thus we gain our word *simony*, which refers to the sale of church
offices.

Vv. 20–23. Peter addressed the magician sharply. "Your silver—may it go with you to perdition!" (author's version). Peter
accused Simon of possessing a wrong intent before God, and
called upon him to repent.

It is difficult to assess Simon's true condition. Peter's reference to perdition may remind one of the fate of Judas Iscariot
("the son of perdition," John 17:12). Yet the words, "You have
no part or portion in this matter," may recall Peter's own ex-

---

81. G. W. H. Lampe, *The Seal of the Spirit* (London: Longmans, Green & Co.,
1951), p. 70, refers to the laying on of hands as "primarily a token of fellowship
and solidarity."

perience in the upper room (John 13:8), pointing to misjudgment but not absence of faith in Christ.

V. 24. Is there a glimmer of hope here? Simon earnestly besought the apostles to intervene with God on his behalf. Or was he simply stricken with the fear of divine punishment? The fact that Luke included no account of God's judgment on Simon may be a positive sign (contra. 13:8–11, the case of Elymas, another magician).

V. 25. Following this, Peter, John, and Philip turned toward Jerusalem, evangelizing as they went through the Samaritan villages. So another territory had been opened to the gospel.

3. Philip and the Ethiopian treasurer (8:26–40)

V. 26. At this point Philip was separated from his ministry with Peter and John and directed by supernatural guidance toward the south—to the road toward old Gaza, the last settlement before the desert to the east of Egypt. The expression *the same is desert* (*hautē estin erēmos*) occurs in geographical descriptions of cities that have been laid waste,[82] but more likely the words refer here to the road, for this would prepare the way for the episode that follows.

Vv. 27–28. The court official—treasurer or chamberlain—represented the queen mother of Ethiopia[83] (probably referring here to Nubia rather than Abyssinia), for the kings of Ethiopia were considered too sacred for normal royal functions. Some scholars have linked this incident with the words of Psalm 68:31: "Envoys will come out of Egypt; Ethiopia will quickly stretch out her hands to God."

If this man was a Gentile, he would be the first such recorded contact in Acts. He may have been on a pilgrimage to Jerusalem to worship at the temple.

As the treasurer journeyed homeward, he occupied his time by reading from a scroll of the Book of Isaiah. The practice in

82. Haenchen, *Acts of the Apostles*, p. 310. The old city of Gaza had been sacked by Alexander Jannaeus in 93 B.C. At this time in history a new city of Gaza had been built closer to the coast.

83. The kings of Ethiopia were regarded as sons of the sun, and the mother of each king was called by the same title, Candace.

antiquity of reading aloud would thus enable Philip to hear him (v. 30).

Vv. 29–31. Philip was directed (by the Spirit in this case) to approach the chariot in which the treasurer was riding. More than this, the man was reading from a remarkable passage in Isaiah, one testifying to Jesus. Philip's question contains an interesting play on words, literally, "Do you understand what you are understanding again" (ginōskeis ha anaginōskeis)?

Replying with his own question, the man asked Philip to be his guide, (lit., "way-shower"; cf. John 16:13, where Jesus said of the Holy Spirit that "He will guide you into all the truth").

Vv. 32–35. This passage from Isaiah is quoted from the Greek text (LXX), the version of the Hebrew Scriptures translated about 250–150 B.C. The passage spoke to the early church of the suffering Servant, who was to be identified with Jesus, even as our Lord Himself had doubtless taught them (cf. Mark 10:45; Luke 24:25–27).

Notice the interesting question on the lips of the treasurer: Did the prophet refer to himself, or to someone else? In choosing among the variety of interpretations put forth, the treasurer seemed to believe the prophet referred to a single person. Nor did Philip hesitate to interpret the passage with reference to the only Person who could fulfill it, and had—Jesus, who "gave His life a ransom for many."[84]

Vv. 36–38. At this point in the journey, the two saw water ahead of them and the new convert requested Christian baptism. According to certain Greek manuscripts,[85] Philip called from the mouth of the man a confession of faith, "Jesus Christ is the Son of God" (see v. 37, KJV). This early creedal statement was probably an addition to clarify the relation of faith and baptism, as though the preaching done by the apostles—repent and be baptized for the remission of sins (Acts 2:38)—was not quite adequate.

Vv. 39–40. The baptismal ceremony completed, Philip was

84. According to John 1:29, Jesus came as "the Lamb of God who takes away the sin of the world."

85. The additional words occur in the Western text (Codex Bezae), then in the Antiochian text, and so into the Textus Receptus and the KJV. See Lake and Cadbury, *Beginnings*, IV, 98.

"snatched away" (*hērpase*) by the Spirit of the Lord, an experience reminiscent of episodes in the lives of Elijah (I Kings 18:12) and Ezekiel (Ezek. 3:14). Once again the Western text reads differently: "The Holy Spirit fell upon the eunuch, and the angel of the Lord snatched away Philip." This reading would match verse 26, where the angel first directed Philip to the south, and would assure the reader that the eunuch received the Holy Spirit (see v. 17).

At any rate, the convert went on his way rejoicing—is this not a mark of the Spirit's presence?—and Philip continued evangelizing in the coastal cities from Azotus (about twenty miles north of Gaza) until he came to Caesarea (which seems to have become his home—see Acts 21:8).

B. The Ministry of Saul Begun (9:1–31)

Saul, with the sight of the martyred Stephen still fresh in his memory, launched his counterattack against the growing church. He determined to root it out wherever he could find the followers of Jesus, and thus set out for Damascus (in Syria) to arrest more men and women. On that journey, an amazing reversal occurred which transformed both the man and his mission.

1. The conversion of the persecutor (9:1–19a)

a. The appearance of the risen Jesus (9:1–9)

This vision became, and continued to be, the central fact of Paul's life. "One must start from it in order to understand Paul, his personality, and his confession."[86]

Vv. 1–2. Still breathing (lit., "breathing in")[87] death threats against the Lord's followers, an atmosphere on which he thrived, the persecutor set out for Damascus. Saul had procured letters of arrest from Joseph Caiaphas, the high priest and head of the Jewish Sanhedrin.

There was a large Jewish community in Damascus, and prob-

---

86. Leo Baeck, *Judaism and Christianity* (New York: Harper & Row, 1966), p. 142.

87. Compare Psalm 18:15 (17:15, LXX), where a similar phrase occurs: *apo empneuseōs pneumatos orgēs sou* ("at the blast of the breath of your anger").

ably some of the disciples had fled there from Jerusalem at the
onset of the persecution, even as some had fled to nearby areas
(Acts 11:19). These people now became known as followers of
"the Way,"[88] a reference to their new way of life.

While the jurisdiction of the high priest seems not to have
reached outside Palestine, in a strict sense, his moral and spiritual influence would doubtless have been widespread. Further,
the Roman authorities generally supported his policies, and ex-
tradition of Jewish offenders was probably demanded in these
letters.[89]

Vv. 3–6. As Saul journeyed toward Damascus he "was laid
hold of by Jesus Christ" (to use his own later explanation of the
experience; see Phil. 3:12). Suddenly a light from heaven flashed
around him; he fell to the ground, and heard a voice calling his
name: "Saul, Saul, why are you persecuting Me?" These phenomena were symbols of a profound spiritual experience. Saul
wrote later of seeing "the light of the gospel of the glory of
Christ, who is the image of God" (II Cor. 4:4). The voice from
heaven is a familiar concept in Luke's record of the early church:
Moses had heard "the voice of the Lord" (Acts 7:31); a voice
from heaven came to Peter during his vision in Joppa (10:13).[90]
The Jewish rabbis referred to the *bath qol*, "the heavenly echo,"
as a way of describing God's voice. On this occasion, however,
the double use of the name—"Saul, Saul"—caught the attention
of the hearer. He heard a penetrating question addressed to the
heart of the matter: "Why are you persecuting Me?" A profound
truth was encased in the question. By persecuting the followers
of Jesus Saul was persecuting the risen Lord! How could that
be? He wrote later that Christ was the "head of the body, the
church" (Col. 1:18), and "we, who are many, are one body in

88. See also Acts 19:9, 23; 22:4; 24:14, 22.

89. In a second-century B.C. letter from Lucius, consul of the Romans, to King
Ptolemy of Egypt, is the following: "If therefore any traitors have escaped from
their country to you, hand them over to Simon the High Priest to be punished
by him according to the law of the Jews" (I Macc. 15:20–21, NEB). A copy was
sent to Simon in Jerusalem.

90. Compare the instances in Jesus' lifetime: at His baptism (Luke 3:22); at
the transfiguration (Luke 9:35); and at His final visit to Jerusalem (John 12:28).

Christ" (Rom. 12:5). Was it on the Damascus road that this great concept was first brought before him?

Now the persecutor had been humbled. He acknowledged the risen Jesus as "Lord" (see Acts 22:10), asking what he should do to serve Him! Saul was now His bondservant, appointed to do His will.

Vv. 7–9. Consternation gripped the company. Those traveling with Saul were rendered speechless, and, while they heard the sound of the voice, they apparently could not distinguish the words being spoken (see Acts 22:9).[91] Saul, blinded by the light, thus was led by the hand into the city. There he remained for three days, sightless and in prayer (accompanied by fasting).

b. The mission of Ananias (9:10–19a)

V. 10. Was Ananias a Damascene, a Jew who had heard the gospel there and had become a follower of the way? Or was he one who had fled from Jerusalem (or Judea) at the beginning of the persecution (see Acts 8:1, 4)? We cannot be certain, but Paul's later description of him seems to favor the former (22:12).

Vv. 11–12. When he was called by the Lord in a vision, Ananias responded. He was told of Saul's condition (praying and blind), was ordered to go to him, and lay his hands upon Saul in order to restore his sight.

Vv. 13–14. Ananias laid an objection before the Lord. He did not doubt the reality of the vision; rather he had a natural fear of going to a man who was a sworn enemy of the followers of Jesus. It was rather like walking into the mouth of a lion!

Word had reached Damascus about Saul and the harm (kaka, lit., "evil") he had done to the Lord's saints in Jerusalem.[92] Further, the persecutor had come to Damascus armed with letters to perpetrate persecution against the Lord's disciples in that city. Understandably, Ananias realized the risk involved.

---

91. Notice the people's response in John 12:29: some said it was the sound of thunder; others that an angel had spoken to Jesus.

92. While the word saints (hagioi) is commonly used in the Pauline letters, in Acts it occurs only in 9:13, 32, 41 and 26:10. C. S. C. Williams, A Commentary on the Acts of the Apostles (New York: Harper & Brothers, 1957), p. 124, suggests that the author of Acts was familiar with Pauline terminology, or even that Paul was Luke's source for this account of his conversion.

Vv. 15–16. Yet the Lord insisted—"Go"! He indicated that Saul was "a chosen instrument of mine"—God's elected servant, to carry His name to the Gentiles as well as to kings and the children of Israel. The apostle later recalled the experience: "[God] was pleased to reveal His Son in me, that I might preach Him among the Gentiles" (Gal. 1:15–16). Even as suffering had been the lot of believers in Jesus at his hands, so Saul would suffer "for My name's sake." And indeed he did, as the Book of Acts (e.g., 14:19; 16:22–24) and his letters show (especially II Cor. 11:23–33; cf. II Cor. 4:8–10; I Thess. 2:2, 15–16).

Vv. 17–19a. Ananias came to Saul where he was residing, laid his hands on Saul, and fulfilled his commission. The newly-converted man received his sight and was filled with the Holy Spirit, "the indispensable qualification for the prophetic and apostolic service"[93] to which he had been called. His baptism followed, which, along with Ananias greeting him as "brother," was a sign of his entrance into the new fellowship.

Possibly a note on Saul's eye condition would be appropriate at this point. Luke—typically interested in bodily conditions—used the phrase, "there fell from his eyes something like scales." The term translated "scales" is *lepides*, which refers to "a flaky substance" or "scaly crusts" on the eyes. In ancient medical usage, the word related to diseases of the skin, not of the eyes. One Jewish source refers to "white patches" on the eyes (Tob. 3:17, NEB); Greek writers refer to "flakes" falling from the skin, but not from the eyes.

2. The commencement of Saul's preaching (9:19b–31)

a. Saul's stay in Damascus (9:19b–25)

Based upon the data supplied by Galatians 1:15–18, we could place this episode within the three-year period specified between Saul's conversion and his visit to Jerusalem (9:26–31). Whether Saul preached in Damascus before he went into Arabia (Gal. 1:17) or after he returned is not clear, although the answer may depend somewhat on the force of the word "immediately" (9:20).

Vv. 19b–20. The length of Saul's stay in Damascus—"for sev-

93. Bruce, *The Book of Acts*, p. 201.

eral days"—is ambiguous, although the phrase probably was intended to stand in contrast to the "many days" of verse 23.

Not now as persecutor, but as proclaimer, Saul went into the synagogues of Damascus (v. 20) heralding the message, "He [Jesus] is the Son of God." Only here in Acts does this title occur, though it is frequent in Paul's letters.

That some Jews of that day related this title to the Messiah is shown by Caiaphas' question addressed to Jesus (see Mark 14:61), and Saul implied the same in his remarks here, saying that "this Jesus is the Christ [Messiah]" (v. 22).

Vv. 21–22. Those who listened to Saul's new message were struck by the obvious contrast between it and the commission with which he had come to Damascus. The word "destroyed" (*porthēsas*), referring to his activity in Jerusalem, is a favorite term in Paul's letters (see Gal. 1:13, 23).

Vv. 23–25. Luke is indefinite about both time and activity; Paul is more specific, at least concerning time, in Galatians 1:17–18. Apparently the total period was three years between Saul's conversion and his return to Jerusalem. During part (perhaps most) of that time he was in Arabia, an area just to the east of Damascus, governed at that time by the noted Nabatean King Aretas IV, who reigned from 9 B.C.–A.D. 40.[94] Possibly Saul engaged in preaching during that stay, for he aroused the ire of the king, whose governor in Damascus sought his life (see Paul's own account of it in II Cor. 11:32–33).

Luke emphasized the Jews' plot against Saul's life. This was the first of many occasions when Saul was opposed by his own people. While the Jews were "watching the gates [of Damascus] day and night" in order to apprehend Saul, the Arabian forces were guarding the city in order to seize him. He was able to slip through them all by escaping by night in a basket[95] let down through the wall of the city. It is interesting that, in listing his many sufferings and narrow escapes, this is the only incident

94. Aretas IV was father-in-law to Herod Antipas, and was angry when Herod divorced his daughter (see Mark 6:17).

95. The "basket" (*spyridi*) was apparently a large, flexible, woven container. The same word occurs in Mark 8:8 in connection with Jesus feeding the four thousand (contrast Mark 6:43 for a word referring to a supply-basket).

he recalled in connection with his whole conversion experience (see II Cor. 11:23–33).

b. Saul's visit to Jerusalem (9:26–31)

Vv. 26–27. In contrast to being befriended by the believers in Damascus, Saul found himself rebuffed by those in Jerusalem. "They were all afraid of him," wrote Luke, for they probably considered him an agent provocateur, seeking to resume his campaign of terror against them.

"But Barnabas. . . ." A happy note is recorded at this point. This man (cf. 4:36–37) was a helper, an encourager, a sympathizer. Later (11:24) Luke called him "a good man"—the Greek word *agathos* showing his beneficence and kindness to those in need.

Barnabas had probably known Saul before this, and seems to have been quite sure of the reality of Saul's conversion. As a man "full of the Holy Spirit" (11:24), Barnabas may have been given the gift of discernment to know the genuine from the pretended (cf. I Cor. 12:10). He retold Saul's experiences before the apostles,[96] vouching for Saul so they would accept him.

Vv. 28–30. Saul's ministry in Jerusalem was at first unopposed. But when he began to argue with the Hellenists,[97] possibly even as Stephen had done (6:9), trouble arose and another attempt was made on his life. At this point the brethren escorted him out of the town to Caesarea, from whence he took ship to his hometown of Tarsus.[98]

V. 31. Is this verse a conclusion to the story of Paul, or an introduction to the story of Peter? Some scholars consider that the departure of Paul, and the cessation of the conflict which

96. In Galatians 1:18–20 Paul swears he saw only Peter and James during his first visit to Jerusalem. Luke's phrase may be a general use of the term "apostles," obviously less specific than Paul's.

97. The term *Hellēnistas* can mean a Greek-speaking Jew (cf. 6:1), a class represented by persons like Stephen, Barnabas, and Paul, or a heathen, as opposed to a Jew. For a full discussion, see Lake and Cadbury, *Beginnings*, V, 59–74.

98. On Tarsus, one of the great cities of the empire, see the Bible dictionaries; the note in Bruce, *Acts of the Apostles*, p. 208; and, particularly, W. M. Ramsay, *The Cities of St. Paul: Their Influence on His Life and Thought* (New York: Armstrong, 1908), pp. 83–244.

his preaching aroused, was the reason for the church experiencing peace. This view would also consider this verse as a concluding "progress report" by Luke (cf. 4:4; 6:7). Others have regarded verse 31 as indicating a summary of Peter's work in Lydda and Joppa (a lengthy report covering 9:32—11:18), showing the growth of the church under his ministry.

C. The Ministry of Peter Concluded (9:32—11:18)

While Luke's earlier story about Peter had been confined to his work in Jerusalem (chaps. 1–6) and a visit to Samaria (8:14–25), the narrative resumes with Peter "traveling through all *those parts.*" He visited Lydda, Joppa, and Caesarea before returning to Jerusalem. During this tour he was instrumental in healing a paralyzed man, raising a dead woman, and proclaiming the gospel to the household of a Roman centurion.

1. In Lydda: Aeneas healed (9:32–35)

V. 32. The "saints" who lived at Lydda,[99] a city between Ashdod and Caesarea, may have been converts of Philip (Philip traveled from Azotus—Old Testament Ashdod—to Caesarea; see 8:40), or people who fled from Jerusalem at the time of Stephen's death (see 8:1).

Vv. 33–35. Was Aeneas a believer? We are not told, but this would not be necessary (cf. 14:8–10, where Paul healed a lame man). Once more Luke was specific about details: the man's name, the length of his illness, and his condition. The healing and the results should be compared with the account in 3:1–11.

2. In Joppa: Tabitha raised to life (9:36–43)

Vv. 36–38. Joppa (Modern Jaffa, the major port on the south coast of Palestine) was the home of a disciple named Tabitha. This is the only occurrence in the New Testament of the femi-

---

99. Lydda has had an interesting history. It was the capital of one of several Jewish provinces, played a role in the Jewish-Roman war of A.D. 66, became a center of rabbinical learning after A.D. 70, was an export center for purple-dyed stuffs, was the site where St. George slew the dragon, and, in the opinion of some, is to be the place of the death of Antichrist.

nine form of "disciple" (*mathētria*, rather than *mathētēs*). Tabitha was noted for her continual deeds of kindness. Just at this time she fell sick and died, and the usual Jewish rite of purification was carried out: "they . . . washed her body." When the believers heard that Peter was nearby, they sent two men (a usual practice in Acts—see 8:14; 11:30; 13:2; 15:27; 19:22; 23:23) to summon him.

Vv. 39–42. Peter, arriving at the house, was taken to the upper room where the body had been laid out. The widows present were probably those who had benefited from Tabitha's good deeds, as is implied by the references to "the tunics and garments" that she had made.

The details of the miracle have a number of similarities to the Markan account of the raising of Jairus' daughter: the people were sent from the room, Peter spoke to the corpse, gave her his hand, and presented her alive to those near to her (cf. Mark 5:40–42).

As at Lydda, the news spread throughout the area and people believed in the Lord.

V. 43. That Peter would lodge with a tanner is noteworthy, for the occupation was considered unclean or defiling by Jewish law. Was it because it was a seaside residence, and Peter, as a former fisherman, would like such a location? Was he showing something of a liberalizing tendency, a characteristic which increased as the story progresses? Was Luke using the incident as a sign of the outreach of the gospel to all kinds of people, whatever their background, culture, or occupation?

3. In Caesarea: Cornelius converted (10)

This is the fullest account of a conversion recorded by Luke, and is repeated in brief in 11:1–18 (where Peter defended his actions) and 15:7–11 (as Peter's testimony at the Jerusalem council). Why was this conversion so vital to Luke and to the early church? It introduced the questions of the salvation of Gentiles, the acceptance of Gentiles into the church, and the social relations between Jewish Christians and Gentiles.

a. Cornelius saw a vision (10:1–8)

Vv. 1–2. Cornelius was a Roman centurion, an officer in charge of one hundred men. Luke mentioned four centurions, two in relation to Jesus' life (Luke 7:1–10; 23:47), one in relation to Peter (Acts 10), and one in relation to Paul (27:1). All gain favorable verdicts. In fact, of the first Jesus said, "I say to you, not even in Israel have I found such great faith."

Luke wrote four descriptive statements about Cornelius: he was a devout man, a God-fearer (a Gentile who had attached himself to the Jewish religion), charitable towards the Jews (cf. Luke 7:5), and one who prayed to God continually. Yet he still awaited the good news of salvation (Acts 11:14).

Vv. 3–6. The vision came in mid-afternoon, a time of prayer (cf. Acts 3:1). An angel appeared, assured Cornelius of God's awareness of his deeds of charity, and urged him to send to Joppa for Simon Peter (to be distinguished from Simon the tanner, with whom Peter was lodging, 9:43).

Vv. 7–8. Cornelius summoned two of his servants and a soldier (described as "devout," as Cornelius had been in v. 2). They were sent to Joppa to bring Peter.

b. Peter saw a vision (10:9–16)

V. 9. While the men were approaching Joppa, Peter went up the roof of Simon's house to pray. The stated times for Jewish prayer were early morning, midday, and the ninth hour (cf. Acts 3:1; 10:3). Illustrations of this practice may be seen in Psalm 55:17 and Daniel 6:10.

V. 10. The words translated "hungry" and "eat" are both of interest. The former appears nowhere else in extant literature except for a quotation in the writings of a first-century physician, Demosthenes. The latter is still used in modern Greek to refer to the midday meal (geuma; comparable to prandium in Rome).[100]

During this time Peter fell into a trance (ekstasis, lit., a condition in which a person "stands outside himself"). Sometimes the word indicates a state of surprise or amazement (cf. Acts 3:10), but it is used again of Paul experiencing a trance (22:17).

Vv. 11–14. Peter saw what appeared to be a great sheet descending from heaven. As the sheet was lowered to the ground he saw it contained all kinds of animals, reptiles, and birds.

100. Bruce, *Acts of the Apostles*, p. 217.

When he was commanded to kill and eat some of them—for it was the noon hour—he strenuously objected: "By no means, Lord." How orthodox he sounded (yet all the while living in a tanner's house)! Later he would understand the words of his Teacher about the problem of "defilement" (see Mark 7:18–19).

Vv. 15–16. As with the prophet Jonah (see Jonah 3:1), the call came the second time, and even a third. Then, as suddenly as the vision had come, it vanished. The lesson Peter was to learn was not simply regarding food, but, more importantly, God's view of people.

c. Cornelius's men brought Peter to the home in Caesarea (10:17–33)

Vv. 17–20. Peter made an attempt to understand the vision. Luke said he "was greatly perplexed" and "was reflecting" on it. At this point the men arrived looking for him, and the Spirit directed Peter to go downstairs and accompany them. The language is similar to the incident concerning Philip (see 8:29).

Vv. 21–23. When Peter inquired of these men the reason for their mission, they replied that their master "was divinely directed[101] by a holy angel" (again, read about Philip, 8:26). Luke appears to be very sensitive to the means by which God guided people in various situations, especially those with an evangelistic flavor.

Vv. 24–26. Not only was Cornelius glad to see Peter when he arrived, but he also fell down before Peter in worship. Peter quickly raised him up, insisting that he, too, was a "human being" (BV; that is, not worthy of homage). For similar examples, see Acts 14:14–15 and Revelation 19:10; 22:9.

Vv. 27–29. Peter acknowledged that it was "unlawful" for a Jew to associate with or visit with a foreigner. The word athemiton indicated all things contrary to God-constituted order for Jewish life, or "breaking a taboo." Thus a man was considered ceremonially unclean, especially if he sat at table with a Gentile

101. See similar uses of the word (echrēmatisthē) in Jeremiah 25:30; 29:23; 30:2; 36:2, 4; Matthew 2:12, 22; Luke 2:26; Hebrews 8:5; 11:7; 12:25. Lake and Cadbury, Beginnings, IV, 117, remark, "The word is used of a divine revelation in all these places. . . . It is similarly used in secular writings."

and shared his food with him. Yet Peter related what God had taught him. The meaning of the vision had now become clear.

Peter's statement that he came "without even raising any objection" is also remarkable, showing that he had been obedient to the Holy Spirit (see v. 20, and 11:12).

Vv. 30–33. Cornelius explained how this all had come about, recounting his experience of the vision (vv. 3–8). He mentioned that he had been praying at the ninth hour when the angel appeared to him; one Greek manuscript (Codex Bezae) adds, "I was fasting. . . ."

d. Peter related the story of Jesus (10:34–43)

Vv. 34–35. Peter's opening statement may have surprised Peter himself after he realized what he had said, true though it was: "God is not one to show partiality," literally, "God has no favorites." The words show that Peter's own Jewish prejudices had been (for this occasion) overcome.[102] Cornelius's works of righteousness, in particular his practice of almsgiving (10:2, 4; cf. Matt. 6:2), had rendered him acceptable to God; this is true of men in every nation. That great truth, uttered by the prophets (cf. Mic. 6:8), had now impressed itself on Peter.

Vv. 36–43. Peter's speech, abbreviated though it may be in its written form, serves as an example of the early apostolic preaching, an observation made earlier by Dodd.[103] The story may be summarized as follows:

1. The word about Jesus prophesied (v. 36)
2. The ministry of John the Baptist (v. 37)
3. Jesus' baptism and anointing with the Holy Spirit (v. 38a)
4. Jesus' ministry: doing good and healing (v. 38b)
5. Jesus put to death on the cross (v. 39)
6. Jesus raised on the third day (v. 40a)
7. Jesus appeared to the disciples (vv. 40b–41)
8. Jesus commissioned the disciples to proclaim His message (v. 42)

102. The word *prosōpolēmptes* occurs here only in the New Testament, and to date is its first known appearance in Greek writings.

103. C. H. Dodd, *The Apostolic Preaching and its Developments* (London: Hodder and Stoughton, 1936), *passim*.

Two things are remarkable about this speech. First, it presents
the ministry of Jesus as *deeds*;[104] nothing is said of His teaching.
Second, the largest proportion is given to the end of His life
(points 5–8), namely, His death, resurrection, appearances, and
commissioning of the disciples.

Further, the order and scope of the speech is a fitting outline
of the content of the Gospel of Mark (it will not fit any of the
other Gospels). This is one of the reasons for the tradition that
the preaching of Peter lies behind the Gospel of Mark.

Jesus is presented as "Judge of the living and the dead," and
one who forgives the sins of everyone who believes in Him.[105]
At this point Peter may have been leading up to an appeal.

Vv. 44–46. Before Peter's message had been concluded, the
Holy Spirit fell upon his hearers. Contrast the earlier situation
when Peter had called upon his listeners to repent and be baptized (2:38). When the new believers spoke with tongues and
exalted God, Peter and his friends were amazed. The Gentiles
had received the same Spirit as the Jewish believers (cf.
11:15–17). Indeed, God was no respecter of persons!

Vv. 47–48. The new converts were baptized in water, and
were recognized to be on the same level before God as the others.
Peter's "Never, Lord" had been turned into a "Yes, Lord." Later
Peter argued from this incident that Gentiles could be saved by
faith apart from the law (15:7–11).

4. In Jerusalem: The church convinced (11:1–18)

There was no little stir within the church in Jerusalem about
Peter's contact with the Gentiles. Peter had to defend his actions.

Vv. 1–3. The word spread rapidly throughout the church in
Judea. When Peter returned to Jerusalem the Jewish Christians
("those who were circumcised") accosted him. The charge? He
had eaten with non-Jews!

Vv. 4–14. Peter's response was a retelling of the events relating to the conversion of the Gentiles. He told of his vision at
Joppa and his call to go to Caesarea. We learn here (v. 12) that

104. Peter said, "He went about doing good." The word *euergetōn* appears
in Luke 22:25 as a title of the kings of the Gentiles: "benefactors."
105. Compare John 5:27 and Mark 2:10.

six brethren (believers) went with him. That would make a total of seven who witnessed the events, a full complement, possibly even an official number (cf. Rev. 5:1, "the seven seals" on an official document).

Vv. 15–18. As Peter recounted the descent of the Spirit upon the Gentiles, he said he recalled the word of the Lord (Jesus) concerning believers being baptized with the Holy Spirit.[106] Thus he understood the reason, and said he could not "stand in God's way."

At this his questioners fell silent. Then they glorified God, acknowledging that He had granted to the Gentiles also repentance to life. The issue, however, would not remain settled for long. In chapter 15, the same issue arose and was debated at the Jerusalem council. To date, however, God had imparted the Spirit to Jews, Samaritans, and Gentiles, showing that He had accepted them all.

106. The prophecy is cited six times in the Gospels and Acts (Matt. 3:11; Mark 1:8; Luke 3:16; John 1:33; Acts 1:5; 11:16); then Paul referred to the baptism in I Corinthians 12:13.

IV. Expansion: To the Remotest Part (11:19—21:14)

Returning to the starting point, that is, the effects of the persecution following Stephen's death (cf. 8:4 with 11:19), Luke next concentrated on the outreach to territories outside Palestine. Included in this section of Acts—following some important preliminaries concerning church leaders—are the three missionary journeys of Paul.

A. The Ministry of Barnabas (11:19–30)

Even as Philip had evangelized in Samaria, and had been followed by the apostles Peter and John (8:5, 14), so certain unnamed persons evangelized territories to the north of Palestine, and were followed, at least in Antioch (Syria), by Barnabas.

1. The church in Antioch established (11:19–26)

Vv. 19–21. Luke recorded the movement of the gospel to the north and west, ultimately to the chief city of the empire (28:30–31). Along with Phoenicia (and its major cities, Tyre and Sidon) and the island of Cyprus, Antioch on the Orontes River was a vital site for evangelism.

Antioch was one of the three chief cities of Rome's sprawling empire (Rome and Alexandria being the others). It had been founded in 300 B.C. by Seleucus Nicator, and became a free city and the capital of the province of Syria under Pompey, after he subjugated it to Rome in 64 B.C. Thence it became the seat of Gentile Christianity, as a large number of its people responded to the gospel.[107]

---

107. In view of Luke's statement, "preaching the Lord Jesus" (11:20), Lake and Cadbury, Beginnings, IV, 129, suggest the evolution of the preaching: first stage—the coming of the kingdom of God and the message of Jesus Himself; second stage—Jesus as the Man ordained to be judge of the living and the dead, and the preaching of the disciples to the Jews; third stage—Jesus as the Lord, extending from Peter's messages to both Jews and Gentiles (i.e., Cornelius) to the preaching to the heathen.

Vv. 22–24. When the news reached the church in Jerusalem, it sent Barnabas as its delegate to Antioch. The choice was excellent for several reasons: Barnabas was a Greek-speaking Jew from Cyprus (just off the coast of Syria), a man marked by sympathy and beneficence ("a good man"), and full of the Holy Spirit and of faith.

As Barnabas saw God's grace upon all, not only those of certain racial or cultural stock, he rejoiced[108] and went about his work of exhorting the converts (cf. 4:36, where he is called "Son of Encouragement"). By word of mouth and by character he showed the power and fruit of the Spirit.

Vv. 25–26. Some years before (probably about ten), Saul had returned to his home city of Tarsus (9:30). After some searching, Barnabas found him and brought him back to Antioch. Thence the two worked together for about a year, teaching those who had been brought to the Lord.

In Antioch the disciples were first commonly known as Christians. The name was originated by the populace of Antioch for this group of people who were distinct from the Jewish inhabitants, and who were known (in all likelihood) as "Chrestians," that is, "those who are kindly people."[109] The name signified a devotee or a partisan in common first-century usage, that is, "a devotee of Christ."[110]

2. The visit to Jerusalem (11:27–30)

Vv. 27–28. During the days when Barnabas and Saul were working in Antioch, prophets made their way from Jerusalem to the new church. One of those prophets was identified by name, Agabus. Luke frequently mentioned people like this in his writings. Beginning with his mention of John the Baptist (Luke 1:76), Luke also used the term of Jesus (Acts 3:22; 7:37),

108. The pun here, in the Greek words *charin* . . . *echarē* ("grace . . . rejoiced"), is intentional. Haechen, *Acts of the Apostles*, p. 366.

109. Only one letter separates the two names, and the *i* and the *e* would have been pronounced similarly. Some scholars take it to be a name given in jest, that is, "the do-gooders." The title *Christ* (Messiah) would have no real meaning to Gentiles.

110. See the extended discussion in Haechen, *Acts of the Apostles*, pp. 367–368.

of Agabus (again in Acts 21:10–11), of several persons at Antioch (13:1), and of the four daughters of Philip (21:9). In the early churches these people appear to have ranked next to apostles (I Cor. 12:28; Eph. 4:11). Agabus prophesied a famine over "the whole world" (the Roman world; cf. Luke 2:1) to come in the days of Claudius.[111] This emperior's reign (A.D. 41–54) was marked by scarcity of food, and the famine seems to have begun in Judea between A.D. 44–48.

Vv. 29–30. A collection was received from each of the disciples who was able to give, and the money was brought together for famine relief (cf. the later incident in I Cor. 16:1–4). The funds were sent in care of Barnabas and Saul, and may be the visit referred to in Galatians 2:1–10, which was "by revelation" (the prophecy of Agabus?). The elders of the church in Jerusalem, rather than the apostles (cf. Acts 6:2–4), received the money from Barnabas and Saul.

B. The Story of Herod's Opposition (12)

1. The arrest and execution of James (12:1–2)

V. 1. This episode ("about that time") may have taken place during the events mentioned in 11:27–30, between Agabus' prophecy and the famine. The king was Herod Agrippa I (A.D. 37–44), grandson of Herod the Great, who, though an Idumean, had endeared himself to the Jews.

V. 2. Herod had James, son of Zebedee, put to death, an act which fulfilled Jesus' prophecy of his future (Mark 10:39). While not mentioned in Acts (aside from 1:13), James had been one of three prominent disciples (Peter, James, and John) named in the synoptic Gospels.

2. The imprisonment and release of Peter (12:3–19)

V. 3. Herod's action proved pleasing to the Jews. At first this seems surprising (cf. Acts 2:47; 5:13; 9:31); yet the Jews had been instrumental in the deaths of Jesus and of Stephen. Thus

---

111. Claudius appears again in Acts 18:2, where his edict expelling Jews from Rome is noted. He was the fourth of the Roman emperors, the nephew of Tiberius and uncle of Gaius.

the conflict flared anew. Some scholars believe this was an attempt on Herod's part to conciliate both Pharisees and Sadducees,[112] and he may have taken advantage of the festival time—the Passover season—to do it.

Vv. 4–5. Luke contrasted what Herod did (put Peter in prison) with what the church did (made fervent prayer to God for him).[113] After the festival Herod intended to bring the prisoner before the people for a public trial. But, as we see, God acted first, and Peter was delivered from his enemies.

Vv. 6–9. While the prisoner was asleep between his guards, an angel of the Lord appeared in his cell, illuminating the darkness (cf. Acts 5:19–20). Peter thought he was seeing a vision, yet he followed the angel's command to gird himself, put on his sandals, and follow him. In the meantime Peter's chains fell off his hands.

Vv. 10–11. The angel led Peter past the guards, through the iron gate leading to the city—as the gate "opened for them by itself"—and went out into the street. Some local color is added to the details by the Western text (Codex Bezae), which inserts, "they went down the seven steps." Many commentators consider the Castle Antonia, at the northwest corner of the temple, to have been the site of Peter's incarceration.

Peter stood alone. The angel had departed. Coming "to himself" is the opposite of being in a trance state ("to be outside oneself"). Then Peter realized that God had delivered him; the prayers of the church had been heard.

Vv. 12–16. For safety and to inform the disciples of his escape, Peter went out at once to the house of Mary, the mother of John Mark. This first mention of the young convert of Peter (cf. I Peter 5:13) introduces the reader to one who was to have an important place in the early church. John Mark was later a companion of Paul and Barnabas and of Peter.

Peter's knock at the door was answered by a servant girl named Rhoda. While she recognized Peter's voice, she could not convince the others (who were still praying for his release!) that

112. Williams, *Commentary*, p. 147.
113. Compare James 5:16: "The effective prayer of a righteous man can accomplish much."

Peter was at the door. Even calling her mad did not dissuade the girl, and when the believers finally answered Peter's persistent knocking, Luke said, they were amazed. Rather than being "his angel"[114] it was Peter himself.

V. 17. Quickly Peter recounted the story, asked the group to report the details "to James and the brethren," and then departed from the city. In view of the death of James the son of Zebedee, this James must be regarded as "the Lord's brother" (cf. Gal. 1:19). He assumed the leadership of the church in Jerusalem at this period (see Acts 15:13; 21:18; I Cor. 15:7; Gal. 2:9) until A.D. 62, when he was murdered. Where Peter went is not known, but we see him still in Jerusalem at the time of the council (Acts 15:13).

Vv. 18–19. In the morning, said Luke, "there was no small disturbance" among the soldiers—"a characteristically Lukan litotes."[115] The situation created great excitement, and following a fruitless search for Peter, Herod ordered the hapless guards executed, or, at least, put under arrest and jailed (cf. Gen. 40:3, LXX).[116]

3. The death of Herod (12:20–24)

V. 20. For some reason, Herod was angry (*thymomachōn*, a participial form which could be rendered "fighting mad," as a modern colloquialism) with the people of Phoenicia. They attempted to regain friendly relations with the king for sound economic reasons.

Vv. 21–23. When Herod arrived at the famous theater in Caesarea, on the special day (possibly in honor of the emperor), he

114. The believers seemed to assume it was Peter's "guardian angel." Compare Genesis 48:16; Matthew 18:10; Hebrews 1:14; and in the Jewish literature, Tobit 5:21. An angel could assume the appearance of his human counterpart.

115. M. Zerwick and M. Grosvenor, *A Grammatical Analysis of the Greek New Testament*, vol. I: Gospels-Acts (Rome: Biblical Institute Press, 1974), p. 391, who give Acts 1:5 as the first example. Haenchen, *Acts of the Apostles*, p. 386, cites a series following this point in Acts: 14:28; 15:2; 17:4, 12: 19:23–24; 27:20. Bruce, *Acts of the Apostles*, p. 248, adds others: 14:17; 17:27; 19:11; 20:12; 21:39; 26:19, 26: 28:2.

116. Codex Bezae reads *apoktanthēnai* ("to be put to death"), rather than *apachthēnai* ("to be led away"), removing the ambiguity.

took his place on the *bēma,* the official judgment seat. As he
announced his reconciliation with the people of Tyre and Sidon,
they hailed him as "of more than mortal nature" (literally), that
is, "a god." When Herod proudly accepted the adulation, he was
struck down by divine judgment. This is a typical Old Testament
expression for interpreting an event as God's judgment, whatever the physical cause may have been (see II Sam. 24:16; II Kings
19:35; II Chron. 13:20). Luke added that Herod was eaten by
worms—a fate, in the ancient world, often imputed to great men
who had offended.[117]

V. 24. In contrast to the fate of Herod, Luke emphasized the
growth of the word of the Lord (cf. 6:7; 19:20).

4. The return of Barnabas and Saul to Antioch (12:25)

Resuming the narrative of 11:27–30, Luke informed his readers of the completion of the mission to relieve the effects of the
famine. Having traveled from Antioch to Jerusalem, and having
delivered the funds, Barnabas and Saul returned to Antioch in
company with John Mark, the son of Mary. This man was also
a cousin of Barnabas (see Col. 4:10).

C. The Ministry of Paul the Apostle (13:1—21:14)

Without question—with or without the powerful support of
Sir William M. Ramsay (*St. Paul the Traveller and the Roman
Citizen*)—Paul was Luke's hero. And it is nowhere more evident
than in this section of Acts. Very soon "Paul" replaces "Saul"
(13:9); the apostle comes into his place of leadership (see 13:13;
"Paul and his companions"); and he moves through travels covering an area of approximately three hundred thousand square
miles. Sensitively, Luke noted the guidance of the Holy Spirit
in the experience of the missionaries and their converts (see
13:2–4, 9, 52; 15:28; 16:6–7; 19:2–6; 19:21 possibly; 20:22–23,
28; 21:4, 11).

1. The commissioning by the Holy Spirit (13:1–3)

V. 1. As was true in the church in Jerusalem, so in Antioch
there were prophets (cf. 11:27; 15:32). "A spokesman [for God]"

---

117. See references in Lake and Cadbury, *Beginnings,* IV, 140. The story of
Herod's fate is graphically told by Josephus, *Antiquities,* 19.8.2.

(translated literally), the true prophet spoke by the Holy Spirit (cf. I Cor. 12:10–11; I Thess. 5:19–20; I John 4:1–2). Teachers too were represented, gifted by the Spirit (cf. John 14:26; Rom. 12:7; I Cor. 12:28).

Little is known of the three others named here with Barnabas and Saul. Simeon was called Niger (probably indicating his African background); Lucius was a Cyrenian (cf. 11:20); Manaen was a member of the court of Herod Antipas (the tetrarch of Galilee and Perea; see Luke 3:1). Saul is mentioned last, possibly indicating his "junior" status at this stage.

Vv. 2–3. The two episodes mentioned here both included prayer and fasting. The former led to the Spirit's call, the latter to a general concurrence with that summons. The word *leitourgountōn* ("while they were ministering") is an expression of special solemnity used in the Greek Old Testament, above all, for prayer,[118] or for the service of God in the temple. In the early church it was used of spiritual exercises, including the collection of money (Rom. 15:27), as well as the general service of God (Rom. 13:6). Thus, while the church at Antioch engaged in serving God in various ways, there came a word from the Holy Spirit, probably through one of the prophets (cf. 11:27). This message called for the separation of Barnabas and Saul for a new work. The fasting may indicate the church's concern for the will of the Lord at this point in service and outreach of the Antiochean congregation.

The Holy Spirit acts sovereignly, designating workers and their work. This was His call—a divine summons. Following more fasting and prayer, the church released these two leaders, laying their hands upon them, and showing their concurrence with God's call.

2. The First Missionary Journey (13:4—14:28)

Two provinces of the empire were visited by the missionaries—Cyprus and Galatia (although Luke did not mention the latter in this case).

118. Haenchen, *Acts of the Apostles*, p. 395; Rackham, *Acts of the Apostles*, p. 189.

a. Cyprus (13:4–12)

V. 4. The missionaries were "sent out" (a stronger word than that describing the church's action in v. 3) by the Holy Spirit. Leaving from the port of Seleucia, they took ship to Cyprus. This island province was placed under senatorial rule, and was governed by a proconsul (see v. 7).

V. 5. Barnabas and Saul arrived at the city of Salamis, a seaport and the chief city of the eastern section of the island. Beginning at this point in Paul's travels, we observe he always began in the synagogue, preaching the gospel "to the Jew first" (cf. 13:46; Rom. 1:16). As many Gentiles (called "God-fearers" in Acts) attended, he had a happy introduction to them as "apostle to the Gentiles."

Accompanying the pair was John Mark, who functioned as a "helper." The word *hypēretēs* refers to an "attendant" (Luke 4:20) or a "minister" (KJV; Luke 1:2). The latter passage is instructive, for it refers to many who handed down the message about Jesus to Luke. Mark was one who wrote a Gospel. Others regard Mark as a teacher or catechist who instructed new converts on the journey through Cyprus; he may have baptized converts.

Vv. 6–7. When the missionaries came to the western end of the island, to Paphos, the capital where the proconsul resided, they met two men: the proconsul, Sergius Paulus, and a Jewish sorcerer named Bar-Jesus. This sorcerer may have been a practitioner similar to Simon Magus (Acts 8:9).

Vv. 8–12. The magician's name is here given as Elymas, probably an interpretation of the word *magos* ("magician"). He opposed the preaching of the gospel to his master, and Saul laid the judgment of God upon him. The apostle was filled with the Spirit and thus able to discern and judge Elymas; Saul "fixed his gaze" upon Elymas. (The term means "a withering look," and is used three times of Paul in Acts, see also 14:9; 23:1; and once of Peter, 3:4.)

At this point (v. 9) the name "Saul" disappears in favor of "Paul." This was possibly the apostle's Roman name (a Roman citizen was given three names at birth), and it was introduced by Luke when Paul set out on his mission to the Gentiles, assumed leadership in the missionary party, and, probably coincidentally, was in the presence of a Roman official bearing the same name.

As a result of all this, the proconsul was amazed and was persuaded to believe in the Lord. Thus, based on the account in Acts, the first Roman officer encountered in Paul's journeys became the first convert.

b. Antioch of Pisidia (13:13-52)

From this point onward, "Paul and his party" is the usual phrase. Paul was the leader, first with Barnabas and John Mark (the latter soon departed), then with Silas, Timothy, Luke, and others (on subsequent journeys).

V. 13. Why John Mark departed at this stage is not revealed,[119] but it is obvious Paul was dissatisfied with the reason (cf. Acts 15:37-39).

Vv. 14-15. Having passed through the coastal province of Pamphylia-Lycia, Paul entered a new, and a crucial, province: Galatia. Here Paul was to found at least four churches, and his later epistle to them was one of the most polemic he ever penned.

While in the synagogue on the Sabbath day, the missionaries were invited to give "a word of exhortation" to the people. This was an expression for the sermon following the reading of the Scripture.

Vv. 16-41. Here is Paul's first speech that was recorded in Acts. It was addressed to an audience of Jews and people who were God-fearers, and centered upon God's grace in sending a deliverer to Israel. We may summarize it as follows.

1. The background in history: God prepared for the coming of Messiah (vv. 17-22)
2. The fulfillment in the present: God sent the Messiah to Israel (vv. 23-37)
3. The appeal to the hearers: God offers forgiveness and justification through Christ to all who believe (vv. 38-41)

---

119. Various ideas have been advanced: Mark was upset by Paul succeeding his cousin as leader of the party; he wanted to stay in Cyprus, which was Barnabas' home territory; he did not want to risk the unknown areas and dangers in Asia Minor; he was smitten by homesickness.

Vv. 17–22. Paul emphasized God's choice of the fathers (Abraham and Jacob, in particular), and His provisions for them in Egypt, the wilderness, and Canaan. The story climaxed with the mention of David, a man after God's heart.

Vv. 23–37. A Savior, Jesus, was the offspring of David. Notice Paul devoted a few words to Jesus' appearance to Israel, a few to His rejection and death, but a long statement to His being raised from the dead (vv. 30–37). (This approach may be compared with the speech of Peter in Acts 2:22–36.) In Acts, the majority of statements about Jesus are centered on His resurrection and its significance.

Vv. 38–41. Forgiveness of sins is proclaimed through Christ (cf. 2:38; 10:43, in conclusions to Peter's speeches). Further, justification ("acquittal," NEB) is offered to everyone who believes, a thing not possible under the Mosaic law. "In other words, Moses' law does not justify; faith in Christ does."[120] Paul's words written to the churches of Galatia, (especially Gal. 2:16; 3:9–14) may be compared with this statement.

Vv. 42–43. The response was positive from many of the hearers—both Jews and proselytes—and Paul urged them to go forward in their newfound relation to God.

Vv. 44–45. The next Sabbath, when the people gathered to hear the word of God, opposition arose from the Jews. "They were filled with jealousy" (the same phrase Luke used in 5:17), and began to contradict and to blaspheme. If the latter word is used as it was in Acts 26:11, it may mean they spoke defamingly of the name of Jesus.

Vv. 46–49. At this point the missionaries announced they were turning to the Gentiles. This was a response to a purely local occurence, rather than a decision based on a theological issue (see 18:6, in Corinth, and 28:28, in Rome, where Paul used the same tactics), for in the very next town, Iconium, Paul entered the synagogue (14:1). Paul cited the prophet Isaiah to show that God intended the Gentiles also to receive the message of salvation.

There is a strong verb regarding eternal life in the words of verse 48. Some commentators have attempted to soften the phrase

120. Bruce, *The Book of Acts,* p. 279.

by translating "appointed" as "disposed." But, as has been observed, the term *tassō* refers to being enrolled or inscribed,[121] relating to names being put into "the book of life" (cf. Luke 10:20; Phil. 4:3). In contrast to unbelievers, those who do believe show that they have been enrolled in God's book. This phrase appears to be a strong statement of predestination, here relating to the Gentiles.

Vv. 50–52. In response to the missionaries' success, the unbelieving Jews raised opposition through loyal women and the city magistrates. The result was an end to the preaching in Pisidian Antioch, for the time being. As Paul and Barnabas left they shook the dust of the city from their shoes (cf. Luke 9:5; 10:11) and went to Iconium. The converts were, however, continually filled with joy and the Holy Spirit (cf. Rom. 5:3–5).

c. Iconium (14:1–7)

Vv. 1–2. Again we see the familiar pattern: the missionaries proclaimed the gospel in the synagogue; "a great multitude" of Jews and Greeks believed; and a disturbance was provoked by Jews who did not believe.

V. 3. A new note is added here. In the face of these conditions, the Lord bore witness to the gospel by granting the working of signs and wonders by the missionaries. Luke frequently called attention to these phenomena, regarding them as showing the coming of the new age (cf. also 4:30; 5:12; 6:8; 7:36; 15:12). Paul claimed these were the signs of a true apostle (II Cor. 12:12).

Vv. 4–7. Things came to a head—the people were divided (some supporting the Jews, others the apostles), and an attempt was made to injure, even to kill the apostles. So they fled into the old district of Lycaonia (now Lycaonia Galatia) for refuge, and entered the cities of Lystra and Derbe, where they continued preaching the good news.

d. Lystra and Derbe and the return journey (14:8–28)

Lystra, like Antioch of Pisidia, had been made a Roman colony in A.D. 6. As a Roman citizen, Paul may have hoped for

---

121. See the references in biblical, intertestamental, and rabbinic sources in Bruce, *Acts of the Apostles*, p. 275; also Bruce's *Book of Acts*, pp. 283–284, n. 72.

some protection here from his persecutors. Yet this turned out not to be the case. This was the only city visited by Paul where there appears to be no evidence of a Jewish synagogue.[122] Probably there were few Jews here, or they may have been assimilated into pagan religion.

Vv. 8–10. Parallels to the story of Peter and the healing of the lame man at the temple (3:2–8) abound. Lake and Cadbury[123] point out the following:

1. the man was lame from his mother's womb (3:2; 14:8)
2. the apostle fixed his gaze on the man (3:4; 14:9)
3. the man leaped up and walked (3:8; 14:10)

In this account it is specified that Paul saw the man had faith to be made well, a feature often present in the accounts of Jesus' healing miracles (cf. Luke 5:20; 7:50; 8:48; 17:19; 18:42).

Vv. 11–14. As a result of this miracle, the people of Lystra hailed the apostles as gods, calling Barnabas Zeus (the chief of the gods of Greece) and Paul Hermes (the god of oratory), for Paul had been doing most of the speaking. Soon the priest of Zeus in the city wanted to offer a sacrifice in their honor.

With this story, and as cultural background for it, we may refer to the Roman poet Ovid's story of Philemon and Baucis.[124] This story, familiar to the people of this area of Asia Minor, may account for their reaction on this occasion—a "second" occurrence! The apostles, reacting as Jews, tore their clothes in horror at this attempted act of worship—blasphemy to them (cf. Mark 14:63).

Vv. 15–18. Paul at once acted to correct the misunderstanding. His speech is the first in Acts addressed to a pagan audience (the case in chapter 10 is no exception, for Cornelius was a worshiper of the God of Israel). The basis of Paul's remarks was

122. While there is no mention of a synagogue in Derbe, the occurrences (see 14:21a) sound much like those mentioned in 13:43 and 14:1. In 16:13, at Philippi, the reference to "a place of prayer" may be virtually synonymous with "a synagogue"; however, as it turned out, there was only a group of women at the riverside (whereas a synagogue service usually required the presence of ten men).

123. Lake and Cadbury, Beginnings, IV, 163.

124. Ovid, Metamorphoses, 8.626ff.

an appeal, not to the Jewish Scriptures, but to the evidences of God in nature. His speech emphasized four things.

1. God is a living being (not a "vain" idol)
2. God is the Creator of all things (cf. Neh. 9:6)
3. He has given men freedom
4. He has given witness of Himself in nature, supplying the needs of His creatures

This is not a distinctively Christian speech, a feature which points strongly to its genuineness. Now that these people had been informed of the true God, they were called to turn to Him in repentance. They had had the gospel preached to them, and were without excuse (cf. Rom. 1:20).

Vv. 19–20. Paul's Jewish opponents followed him from Antioch and Iconium to Lystra and persuaded the people against him. The stoning appears to have been a mob action, rather than a judicial proceeding. Paul referred to it in II Corinthians 11:25 and indirectly, years later, in II Timothy 3:11.

One is hard put to know whether Luke intended to imply the miraculous here: was Paul only stunned by the stones, then regained consciousness? Or was he done to death, then resuscitated? Luke's tendency in Acts was to not emphasize Paul's sufferings (Haenchen), and even accounts about miracles were often treated with restraint. In any case, under his own power, Paul was able to walk back into Lystra, and the next day walk to Derbe (a distance of about thirty miles).

Vv. 21–23. The return visit—through Lystra, Iconium, and Antioch—completed the mission to Galatia. During this time the missionary strategy of Paul is clearly seen: evangelizing, followed by teaching (vv. 22), and organizing the churches by appointing elders (v. 23). To this extent Paul left each group on a fairly solid footing and urged them to carry on, although there would be tribulations. But the apostles commended the believers to the Lord (cf. John 16:33).

Vv. 24–28. Preaching as they journeyed, Paul and Barnabas soon arrived in Antioch (Syria), from which point they had been commended to their work. Then occurred a kind of missions conference, at which time they reported on all that had been done. The great note of joy was that God "had opened a door of faith to the Gentiles." The new era in missions had begun.

3. The Jerusalem council (15:1–35)

This was a meeting of great moment; the question at hand was not a matter of mere personal interest. Rather, the very heart of the issue was the nature of salvation. To put it bluntly, what did a person have to do; what kind of response to God was required? In more practical terms, how was one recognized as a member of the church, and what was the basis of social inter-course between peoples of differing backgrounds? Jewish Christians (mainly from Jerusalem) were insisting on the necessity of the rite of circumcision, not simply a recognition of its symbolic meaning. Yet this had not been insisted on in churches such as Antioch; not even the Gentile Cornelius was refused acceptance (Acts 10:47; 11:17–18).

Also, there had been cases of confusion on the part of some of the apostles. The account of Peter's hypocrisy, affecting even Barnabas (Gal. 2:11–13), was a case in point. If this incident is properly dated following the First Missionary Journey, when Paul and Barnabas returned to Antioch (14:27–28) and prior to the council, it provides a specific example of the problem.

The apostolic decree (15:19–20, 28–29) was an attempt to settle these two questions: how are Gentiles saved, and how can Jewish and Gentile Christians manage to live in harmony?

a. The occasion (15:1–5)

V. 1. Notice the contrast between the statement about salvation here with the close of the previous narrative (14:27). Added to "faith" was the demand for circumcision. In other words, these teachers said that one first had to become a Jew before he could become a Christian.

Vv. 2–4. After much discussion between the brethren from the church in Judea and Paul and Barnabas, it was decided a delegation be sent to Jerusalem to discuss the question with the apostles and elders. As Paul and Barnabas went they spread the word about the salvation of the Gentiles, and were received by the leaders in Jerusalem.

V. 5. The statement of the believing Pharisees is quite under-

standable in view of their background. Even as Jesus was the
Messiah out of Israel, so Christianity was Judaism brought to its
completeness, and salvation was the special heritage of the chosen nation, offered on sufferance to those who came under the
shadow of Israel.[125]

b. *The witnesses and the decision (15:6–21)*

Vv. 6–9. After the leaders of the church assembled to discuss
the issue, Peter was the first to speak, recalling the earliest experiences of the Jerusalem church. He had been God's choice to
take the gospel to Gentiles, and God, making no distinction,
imparted the Holy Spirit to those who believed. Gentile along
with Jew had been accepted by God; why should men make any
further requirement?

Vv. 10–11. Peter exhorted the elders not to lay a yoke upon
the necks of these Gentile converts. What was this yoke? In a
related statement, Paul referred to "a yoke of slavery" (Gal. 5:1),
describing the character of legal requirements for salvation, a
thing from which Christ set people free. The word refers to a
burdensome requirement, something too heavy to bear (cf. Matt.
23:4). By contrast, Peter argued, both Jew ("we") and Gentile
("they") are saved "through the grace of the Lord Jesus." In
saying this, Peter was not so much imitating Paul as asserting
that the Jerusalem church agreed with the principle of Paul's
preaching (cf. Gal. 2:9).

V. 12. The weighty testimony of Peter brought silence to the
group and the elders listened to Barnabas and Paul[126] as they
related how God had given evidence of His approval of their
ministry among the Gentiles (see 14:3). As their story is familiar
to the reader from the previous narrative (chaps. 13–14), Luke
had no need to repeat the details here.

Vv. 13–18. James, generally identified as the brother of Jesus
(cf. Gal. 1:19; 2:9), acted as president of the council. He con-

125. J. C. Macaulay, *A Devotional Commentary on the Acts of the Apostles*
(Grand Rapids: Eerdmans, 1946), p. 166.
126. Notice the order of the names reverts to the earlier period, when Barnabas had been the delegate of the Jerusalem church to Antioch, and the first
recognized leader of the mission to the Gentiles (in other words, before Acts
13:9).

firmed the logic of the former witnesses, and argued that God indeed had done something new. Added to Peter's testimony is that of the prophets (Amos, in particular).

God had come among the Gentiles to claim "a people (*laos*) for His name." A paradox, indeed, for in the LXX the word *laos* is generally used to describe Israel, God's chosen ones, in distinction from the Gentiles (*ethnē*). Thus the new people of God is to be composed of both Jew and Gentile. As support for this James cited Amos 9:11–12. James cited the words of the LXX version of Amos, and this differs in a number of respects from the Hebrew text. Most importantly, the LXX uses the phrase "that the rest of mankind may seek the Lord," rather than the Hebrew, "that they [Israel] may possess the remnant of Edom." This applies the prophecy to the new situation, instead of to the restoration of the house of David over the territory included in David's kingdom.

Vv. 19–21. In verses 19–20, two separate issues were considered. First, the council decided that the Gentiles must be allowed to come to God on the basis of faith and His free grace. This is the same principle expounded at length by Paul in Galatians and Romans. Second, the problem of social relations between Jewish and Gentile believers had to be faced. The decision was to ask the Gentile believers to respect the scruples of their Jewish brethren in certain areas: food dedicated to idols; illicit sexual relations; meat from which the blood had not been drained; and drinking blood. All of these were regarded as ceremonially defiling by Jews,[127] and had antecedents in the Scriptures.[128] Such concessions would not injure Jewish standards, James contended, for the law of Moses was consistently taught in the synagogues, so that biblical teaching would confront people wherever they were found.

c. *The letter to Antioch (15:22–35)*

V. 22. To accompany Paul and Barnabas back to Antioch two

---

127. The Western text contains a reading changing the decree to moral rather than ceremonial issues: "idolatry, fornication, and blood" are to be avoided, and adds, "do not do to others what you would not like done to yourselves," a form of the so-called Golden Rule.

128. Compare Exodus 34:15; Leviticus 17:10, 13–14; 18:6–18, 28. Harrison, *Acts*, pp. 235–236, suggests that the item regarding fornication might better be understood as various kinds of unlawful marriages (as in Lev. 18).

leaders from Jerusalem were selected: Judas Barsabbas and Silas. Of the former we hear nothing more; the latter apparently became the traveling companion of Paul (15:40; cf. II Cor. 1:19; I Thess. 1:1; II Thess. 1:1) and later of Peter (I Peter 5:12).

Vv. 23–29. The letter explained the circumstances of the decision concerning the relations between Jews and Gentiles. This decision, the church believed, was initiated by the Holy Spirit, and the church functioned as His vehicle ("For it seemed good to the Holy Spirit and to us"). The language reminds the reader of that same kind of awareness described earlier (cf. 13:2–3).

Notice the tone of the letter. It is free from harshness or dictatorial speech. Rather we sense the language of genuine concern and a plea for unity among the believers. The same attitude may be seen in such passages as Romans 14:1ff and I Peter 4:7–11.

Vv. 30–35. Both the letter and the prophetic ministry of Judas and Silas were of great encouragement to the church in Antioch. When these two men returned to Jerusalem, they had been sent in a state of peace. The church was then strengthened further by the word of the Lord being ministered by Paul, Barnabas, and many others in Antioch.

4. The Second Missionary Journey (15:36—18:22)

This journey, like the first, centered in two provinces, Macedonia and Achaia (parts of modern Greece). As he traveled to these areas, Paul visited the churches along the way, including the cities of Galatia.

a. The dissension between Paul and Barnabas (15:36–41)

Vv. 36–39. When Paul suggested a visit to the churches founded on the first journey, Barnabas suggested taking John Mark with them again. Paul dissented, claiming Mark had deserted them earlier, and had failed in his role in the mission.

The disagreement between Paul and Barnabas was sharp—Luke's word is *paroxysmos* (cf. 17:16 for the verb form—"being provoked"), and while Luke assigned no blame to either party, a separation between the two missionaries was the result. Instead of harming the mission, their parting actually doubled the work force. Barnabas and Mark went to Cyprus, while Paul and Silas went northward.

Vv. 40–41. A strong link was forged between Paul and the
Jerusalem church by his choice of Silas (cf. 15:22, 32). Further,
Silas, like Paul, was a Roman citizen, which was another ad-
vantage in their work. They, being commended by the brethren,
began their new mission among the churches of the province
Syria-Cilicia.

It is notable that after this point Barnabas and John Mark are
not mentioned again in Acts. From this point the story is wholly
concerned with the career of Paul, first as itinerant missionary
and later as a prisoner of the Roman government.

b. Galatia (16:1–5)

Vv. 1–3. Coming into the cities of South Galatia, Paul gained
an additional member in his party. Timothy came highly rec-
ommended by the believers of the local churches in Lystra and
Iconium. He was the son of a mixed marriage—a Jewish mother
and a Gentile father.[129] We learn, too, that Timothy's mother,
Eunice, was a woman of strong faith (she was probably a convert
of Paul's on the first journey), and that Timothy had been introduced to the Scriptures as a child (II Tim. 1:5; 3:14–15).

As Timothy had been reared by a Jewish mother, he was,
practically, a Jew; probably, because his father was a Greek, he
had not received the rite of circumcision. Thus Paul felt it wise,
to avoid an additional problem in the ministry to Jews of the
Dispersion, to have Timothy circumcised. Since Timothy had
been reared in the Jewish faith it seemed to Paul expedient to
take this precaution. Based on his principle of conciliation in
matters which would violate no principle of his faith (see I Cor.
9:19–22), Paul was willing to take a step which indeed has
brought criticism to him.

Vv. 4–5. Paul and Silas delivered the decrees of the Jerusalem
council as they went through the cities of Galatia. These churches,
while outside the stated scope of the letter (15:23), had been
evangelized on the first mission, originating from Antioch. Thus

129. While some writers deny the possibility of such a marriage (see Haenchen,
Acts of the Apostles, p. 478, n. 3), others assure us "there can be little doubt that
the Jews married into the dominant families" (of Asia Minor). William M. Ramsay,
The Bearing of Recent Discovery on the Trustworthiness of the New Testament
(London: Hodder and Stoughton, 1915; reprint ed., Grand Rapids: Baker, 1979)
p. 357.

Paul apparently felt a responsibility to inform them.[130] This visit brought further progress in the work of the Lord in Galatia; the churches were being strengthened and growing.

c. Troas (16:6–10)

Vv. 6–8. The sure meaning of Luke's words in verse 6 has not been discovered, particularly the meaning of the expression "the Phrygian and Galatian region."[131] In other words, by what routes did Paul make his way from the South Galatian cities until he finally arrived at Troas, on the coast of Asia Minor? Did he visit "North Galatia" (the usual meaning of the name *Galatia* in classical times)? Or did he go into the province of Asia on the way, although he was not permitted to preach? These and other questions still remain even after much discussion.

Two things do stand out as far as Luke's account is concerned. First, the account is very brief, considering the size of the territory involved; nor did Luke record any preaching missions along the way. We see that Paul usually followed main roads in his travels, and there were such roads running both north and northwest from Antioch (Pisidia). Second, the account is marked by emphasis upon the guidance of the Spirit. Paul was forbidden to speak the word in Asia (he may have had Ephesus in mind) or to enter Bithynia (a province on the northern edge of Asia Minor). While we do not learn what means the Holy Spirit used, we see that Paul was spiritually sensitive, and followed the orders of the Spirit of Jesus (the risen Lord).

Vv. 9–10. The city of Alexandria Troas was a major port on the coast of Asia Minor (modern Turkey), and had been given the status of a Roman colony by the emperor Augustus (27

130. While Paul did mention the decree in this visit to Galatia, he made no use of it in his contacts with the questions regarding food in either Corinth (see I Cor. 8–10) or Rome (see Rom. 14:1–15). This was probably due to the different circumstances in these churches, particularly the libertine elements there present.

131. Some of the classic discussions, aside from those in commentaries on Acts, are William M. Ramsay, *The Church in the Roman Empire before A.D. 170* (New York: Putnam, 1893); Lake and Cadbury, *Beginnings,* V, pp. 231–239; G. Ogg, *The Chronology of the Life of Paul* (London: Epworth, 1968); and W. M. Calder, "The Boundary of Galatic Phrygia," in *Proceedings of the Orientalist Congress* (Istanbul, 1951), in which Lake's position is countered successfully, according to Bruce, *The Book of Acts,* p. 326, n. 15.

B.C.–A.D. 14). Here Paul received a vision during the night. No
doubt at this juncture he must have been wondering about the
next step in his missionary program. The call of God, as the
missionaries discerned the next morning, was given by the appearance of a man of Macedonia in Paul's vision, and the man
entreated (*parakalōn*) Paul, "Come over to Macedonia and help
us." This may be an instructive example of guidance for the
believer. Taking verses 6–10 as a unit, we see the following
factors: the missionaries had been commended to the work of
the Lord (15:40); after they finished the work in Galatia, two
other doors had been closed to them (vv. 6–7); after coming to
Troas, by one of the main roads, they came to the sea, and thus
had two options: either cross the sea, or return to their home
base; the vision was a direct call to cross over to Macedonia.

The party listened to Paul's account of the vision the next
morning, and determined to set out for Macedonia, "concluding" (*symbibazontes*) God had called them. The word literally
means to "add" or "put together." After considering the various
factors, of which the vision was the climax, the group felt sure
of divine direction to preach the gospel.

Notice, finally, that in this passage the familiar "we" sections
of Acts commence (although Codex Bezae has the plural pronoun at Acts 11:28, probably based on the tradition of Luke as a
native of Antioch). This continues until 16:17, then resumes in
20:6, where "we sailed from Philippi" (apparently Paul had left
Luke there for a period of several years), until 21:18, when the
group reached Jerusalem. The final section begins in 27:1 and
concludes in 28:16, when the missionaries arrived in Rome.

d. Philippi (16:11–40)

Obviously Luke had an interest in Philippi. This seems ap-
parent from the length of the narrative, the description of the
city (v. 12), and the sampling he gave of the incidents involving
Paul.

Vv. 11–12. It was a two-day sail from Troas, past Samothrace,
the five-thousand-foot mountain in the Aegean Sea, to Neapolis,
the seaport of Philippi. For siding with the victorious Octavian
(later the emperor Augustus) in 42 B.C., Philippi was given the
status of a Roman colony. This meant its constitution and lead-

ership were modeled on that of the mother city. Luke called Philippi "a leading city" of the province, and it was located in the first, or eastern, district of Macedonia.

Vv. 13–15. On the Sabbath day the missionaries, looking for a synagogue, went outside the city to the river Gangites (or Angites). (It is not clear why they chose to look for a meeting place in this location.) While they found no synagogue, the results were rewarding, for out of the women (the "man of Macedonia" never appears in the narrative!) who met there was garnered the first European convert to the gospel (in Paul's ministry).

Lydia, a businesswoman from the city of Thyatira, in the province of Asia (cf. Rev. 2:18–29), was, like Cornelius (10:2), a Gentile who worshiped the God of Israel. Now she, too, was being called to faith in the Messiah; the Lord opened her heart to respond to the gospel. She and her household were baptized and gave hospitality to the missionaries. (Notice also Paul's reference to leading women in the church at Philippi in Phil. 4:2–3.)

Vv. 16–18. A second incident concerned the slave girl through whom a spirit spoke—Plutarch called such persons "ventriloquists." By telling fortunes this girl had brought her masters much business.[132] Following the missionaries about (did she detect a higher level of spirituality?), she kept crying out that these men, as servants of "the Most High God," proclaimed "the way of salvation." Both these expressions were used among Jews and pagans as well, thus providing a common ground for clarifying the true meaning of the words. Paul was bothered by the clamor and, turning, rebuked the spirit in the name of Jesus Christ. The spirit departed at once, giving peace to all concerned.

Vv. 19–24. Angry over their loss of profit, the masters of the girl dragged Paul and Silas before the city authorities. Paul's other companions, Timothy and Luke, were not arrested, possibly due to their lack of prominence in the incident; possibly Paul and Silas were seized because they were Jews (cf. v. 20).

The charges were slanted toward gaining favor with the Roman rulers: these Jews were proclaiming customs unlawful to

---

132. Some scholars prefer the translation "much profit" here, and in 19:24.

Romans. This is a good example of the pride of Roman citizenship in that period of history.

After the magistrates' police attendants beat them with rods (cf. v. 35), a punishment Paul suffered at least three times (II Cor. 11:25), the missionaries were thrown into prison, and found themselves fastened by their feet into the stocks.

Vv. 25–26. This incident led to the conversion of a third person in Philippi—the jailer himself. The contrasts between these converts are striking: a religious, devout person; a girl, unfortunate and exploited; and a Roman soldier. These are not unlike the examples of persons selected by John early in Jesus' ministry (cf. John 3–4): a religious leader, Nicodemus; the woman of Samaria; and an officer of Herod's court.

Despite the missionaries' ill-treatment, the praise of God within their hearts came forth in song, and at midnight the jail was filled with a joyful duet. Suddenly an earthquake rocked the foundations, causing the doors to spring open and chains to fall from the walls. Once again God had produced a miraculous circumstance in a moment of need (cf. 5:19; 12:6–7).

Vv. 27–31. The jailer, suddenly roused from sleep, viewed the situation with alarm. Surely all the prisoners had escaped. Thus his one thought was suicide (for he would be held accountable for his prisoners). Paul, with a loud cry, dissuaded him— and the man responded to the uncanny circumstances by calling to Paul and Silas, "Sirs, what must I do to be saved?"

The jailer's question had been interpreted in one of two ways: with reference to his physical life—how he could avoid being executed for (as he thought) failing as a soldier; with reference to his spiritual life. If the latter was the case, he may have heard what the slave girl had proclaimed (see v. 17), or what the missionaries had been saying or singing in the jail. In any case, Paul directed his answer toward the jailer's spiritual need: "Believe in the Lord Jesus." The good news would bring salvation to him and to his household (see also Acts 11:14 for the same expression).

Vv. 32–34. The word of the Lord was declared to the whole household, and the people responded and were baptized. Also, the jailer washed the wounds of the two missionaries (what a

contrast to the earlier beating), and then everyone rejoiced together in his house at the newfound salvation.[133]

Vv. 35–40. The same men who had beaten Paul and Silas (vv.
22–23) were sent by the magistrates the next morning to declare
the missionaries' release from jail. The vagrants had been taught
their lesson! But Paul objected. An illegal beating and jailing
could not be dismissed so casually. He demanded the magistrates appear personally. The charge against Paul and Silas had
not been verified. Thus the beating and jailing were violations
of Roman law (for both men were Roman citizens, v. 37). With
apologies and possibly fears of public reaction, the magistrates
begged Paul and Silas to leave the city.[134]

Possibly the incident worked out to the advantage of the
church in Philippi. The officials, at least, may have had more
respect for the group of believers than if their founder had been
a convicted felon.

Soon the missionaries left the city, after exhorting the church
(cf. 14: 22). Luke stayed behind; Paul, Silas, and Timothy made
their way toward Thessalonica. The history of this church is one
of the happiest in the New Testament (cf. Phil. 1:3–6; 4:14–19).

e. Thessalonica (17:1–9)

Vv. 1–3. Thessalonica lay on the Via Egnatia; Paul traveled
that famous road from Philippi through Amphipolis (the capital
of the first district of Macedonia) and Apollonia. Thessalonica
was made the capital of the province of Macedonia in 146 B.C.,
and was a free city. Thus its government was in form demo-
cratic, and its chief rulers were called politarchs (lit., "city-
rulers").[135]

Here, in the synagogue, Paul "reasoned" (*dielexato*) with the
Jews, attempting to show from the Scriptures that Jesus indeed

133. St. Chrysostom commented about the jailer: "He washed them, and he
was washed; he washed them from their stripes, he himself was washed from
his sins" (*Homer*, 36.2), cited in Harrison, *Acts*, p. 257.

134. The magistrates could not expel Paul and Silas, who were Roman citizens and uncondemned, so they requested that the missionaries leave.

135. The title was inscribed on an arch before the city, and has also been
discovered in inscriptions from Macedonia.

was the Messiah.[136] This is the first use of the word "reasoned" in Acts, but it appears as descriptive of Paul's approach to the people in every major city from this point through his third journey—in Athens, Corinth, Ephesus (three times), and Troas.[137] These were all Greek cities (either on the mainland or the Ionian coast), and this method of communicating was typically Greek, having been the special characteristic of Socrates. The term may refer to discussion by means of question and answer, to reasoning or arguing, or, as we might say today, to dialogue.[138]

Vv. 4–5. As was true of the experience in Pisidian Antioch (cf. 13:43–45), there was a dual response here: acceptance and opposition. Later, references occur in one letter to Thessalonica which may reflect on these incidents (I Thess. 1:6; 2:14–16).

Vv. 6–9. The charge against the missionaries, leveled by the unbelieving Jews and the mob, was a serious one: they had fomented revolt. The word "upset" (see also 21:38, again involving Paul) may also mean "to stir up sedition." This word is found in the papyri with reference to a boy, who, by his bad conduct, had upset his mother.[139] Further, the missionaries had also, it was charged, spoken against Caesar by saying there was "another king," namely, Jesus.[140] Paul's preaching had referred to Jesus as God's Son, and referred to Him coming from heaven in judgment against mankind (cf. I Thess. 1:9–10; 2:19; II Thess. 1:7–8), a message that could easily be interpreted in a seditious sense.

A man named Jason, not otherwise identified, had given hospitality to the missionaries, and seemingly had put up security or bond against any repetition of such disturbances. This may

136. That the Messiah had to suffer and die, and rise again from the dead, was a frequently-repeated concept in the early Christian preaching. See Peter's words (Acts 3:18; I Peter 1:11); Paul's (Acts 26:23; I Cor. 15:3–4); and the Lord's words to His disciples (Luke 24:26, 46).

137. Acts 17:17; 18:4, 19; 19:8–9; 20:7, 9.

138. See Rackham, *Acts of the Apostles*, pp. 294–295.

139. See Adolph Deissmann, *Light from the Ancient East* (reprint ed., Grand Rapids: Baker, 1978), for more about the word *upset*, and the letter in the papyri, pp. 85, 201–204.

140. Compare Luke 23:2.

have been the reason Paul could not return (cf. I Thess. 2:18), an action attributed to satanic activity.

f. Berea (17:10–15)

Vv. 10–11. Contrast the reception here with the situation in Thessalonica. The Jews of Berea listened to Paul, then diligently searched the Scriptures in order to see whether his teachings were biblical. The term "noble," referring, literally, to "good birth," came to mean "free from prejudice," "liberal," or "generous."

Vv. 12–15. Not surprisingly, many Jews believed, again with a number of Greeks. But soon the word got back to Thessalonica, and the Jews there came to Berea, stirred up the people, and, as a result, Paul was hurried out to the Aegean Sea, from whence he made his way to Athens. Silas and Timothy, apparently not objects of attack, remained for a while longer.

g. Athens (17:16–34)

Two scenes dominate this part of Luke's narrative: Paul in the marketplace (agora) of Athens, and before the Areopagus. This is the only city in which Paul preached without an uprising of some sort.

Vv. 16–17. Paul had arrived in the leading city of Greece, a place representing the highest level of culture known to classical antiquity. Never surpassed were the sculpture, the literature, and oratory of Athens in the fifth and fourth centuries B.C., and she led the field also in philosophy—the names of Socrates, Plato and Aristotle, Epicurus and Zeno (these in the later period, about 300 B.C.) represent man's magnificent intellectual attainments.

Why was Paul's spirit being provoked (cf. 15:39) at these sights [141]—a city "full of idols"? Certainly the modern Christian may not view the art in the same way. As a Jew, Paul had been reared on the words of the Decalogue: no other gods and no graven images (Exod. 20:3–4). To Paul there was one God, and one Lord (I Cor. 8:6); the pagan gods were "by nature . . . no gods" (Gal. 4:8); the idols represented demon forces (I Cor. 10:20).

141. Lake and Cadbury, Beginnings, IV, 210, refer to the agora of Athens as "a forest of statues with buildings on all sides."

This provocation led him to take up dialogue with the Athenians, both in the synagogue and in the marketplace.

Vv. 18–20. The Epicurean and Stoic philosophers were the popular street philosophers of the day, emphasizing ethics above theoretical ideas. Epicurus (341–270 B.C.) had founded a movement emphasizing pleasure—a life devoid of pain, fear, and disturbing desires; a life of tranquillity. The fear of death had been abolished by Epicurus, for he taught that the gods cared not about humankind, and that death was the end.

Zeno (340–265 B.C.) founded a school (called Stoic because they often met in the Stoa Poikile, "the painted portico") emphasizing life in conformity with nature; virtue (meaning to live rationally) was the highest good. In contrast to the Epicureans, this school taught the value of pain, hardship, and justice—to avoid these were signs of weakness.

Some listeners called Paul an "idle babbler," a translation of *spermalogos*, literally, "one who picks up seeds or scraps." First applied to a bird ("cock sparrow") which picked up grain, the word came to mean people who picked up ideas of any kind and casually passed them on to their listeners.[142] Others regarded Paul as a proclaimer of "strange deities" (or "new" gods, v. 18), even as Socrates had been described in 399 B.C.[143] Who were these "strange deities"? Presumably "Jesus" and "resurrection," which may reflect the personification of healing and "recovery."[144]

Paul was brought to the Areopagus—a name given both to a place ("Mars' Hill") in Athens and to a court (which in early Greek history met on the hill). This court governed religious matters in the city, and may thus have been concerned about the teachings of the apostle.

V. 21. This Lukan note, according to ample testimony, is

142. *Ibid.*, p. 211.

143. " . . . who does not believe in the gods of the state, but has other new divinities of his own," Plato, *Apology*, from *Dialogues*, in *Great Books*, vol. 7, p. 203, sec. 24.

144. The Greek word for healing, *iasis*, is similar to the name Jesus, *Iēsous*; the Greek word for resurrection, *anastasis*, may have been regarded as the name of a goddess, or have been related to the idea of recovery or renewal, together with the idea of healing.

"the simple truth" (Blaiklock). "Something new" translates *ti kainoteron,* which might also be rendered "the newest of all," or, more colloquially, "the latest thing." The Athenians were known for their insatiable curiosity.

Vv. 22–23. The opening of Paul's speech, the words of which are today inscribed on a bronze plate at the foot of the Areopagus, is remarkably conciliatory. Paul referred to the religious character of the Athenians, and to their worshipful attitude toward "an unknown god." By their devotional approach they wanted to ensure safety for their city from all possible harm, taking care not to overlook any deity.

Vv. 24–31. Paul's doctrine of God was presented from several vantage points:

1. God as Creator (v. 24)
2. God as self-sufficient (v. 25)
3. God as ruler of the earth and sustainer of life (vv. 26–28)
4. God as judge of mankind (vv. 29–31)

Throughout the speech, Paul made an effort to work from common ground.[145] He "was eager to grasp the opportunity to write the name of the God he knew upon that anonymous altar."[146]

As Creator, God is Lord of heaven and earth (cf. Gen. 1:1). This concept of creation is deeply rooted in the Old Testament (e.g., Ps. 19:1–6; Isa. 40:12–28; 44:24), and was distinct from Greek views in at least two respects: the Supreme Being was also Creator, and creation was not done by a demiurge; the Creator brought all things into existence, and matter was not eternal. As Creator, God is self-sufficient, not dependent on His creatures (cf. Job 35:7; 41:11), and ministers to all life and breath, showing His nearness to them.

The race has sprung from one man, Adam (cf. Rom. 5:12), a concept not congenial to Greeks, who believed they had a native origin and felt superior to non-Greeks. And God had determined the boundaries of human habitation (cf. Deut. 32:8). Mankind is dependent on Him for very life, for the creature is the product

145. Bruce, *Acts of the Apostles,* p. 336.
146. Harrison, *Acts,* p. 270.

of the hand of the Creator. These last words (v. 28) appear to echo the words of Greek poets—first, possibly Epimenides the Cretan (cf. Titus 1:12), then Aratus (in his *Phainomena*), a Stoic.[147]

Finally, Paul stressed that God stands as Judge, and called for all to repent. God has given notice of a coming day of judgment by appointing a man to carry out that role (cf. Dan. 7:13; John 5:27), a note that Peter had earlier sounded to a non-Jewish audience (Acts 10:42). This man God had raised from the dead, a prelude to and proof of the coming day.

Notice, throughout the speech, how Paul kept as close to his hearers as possible, yet used the revelation of the Scriptures to lay bare their ignorance of God and His ways. At one time Paul thrust against the Epicureans (e.g., vv. 27–28), at another against the Stoics (e.g., vv. 28b, 31). But there is a final thrust at both with the reference to resurrection of the dead, an idea repugnant to them all.

Vv. 32–34. Some began to sneer (Epicureans?), while others suggested further conversation (Stoics?). The former denied both resurrection of the body and immortality of the soul, while the Stoics believed the soul lived on. Yet others believed, including Dionysius (a member of the court of the Areopagus), a woman named Damaris, and other unnamed persons, quite a heartening response in an address to the intelligensia of Athens. To all who doubt whether Paul preached the gospel in Athens, a reading of verses 18 and 34 should be adequate.

h. Corinth (18:1–17)

V. 1. Following his visit to Athens, Paul traveled fifty miles to the southwest to the famous commercial center of Corinth. The city which he saw had been rebuilt in 46 B.C., a hundred years after its destruction by the Roman general Mummius. Julius Caesar established it as a Roman colony, and in 27 B.C. it became the capital of the province of Achaia. With its two ports, Lechaeum on the west and Cenchrea (cf. Rom. 16:1) on the east, Corinth was a shipping center. In classical times (pre-146 B.C.) it had a reputation for immorality—the famous temple of Aphrodite, goddess of love, being a center of religious prosti-

147. These words from Aratus are found also in the *Hymn to Zeus*, a poem by Cleanthes, another Stoic poet.

tution. In those days, at least, "to act the Corinthian" was a reference to practicing sexual immorality.

Vv. 2–3. The pair who Paul met here, Aquila and Priscilla, proved to be among his best friends and earnest fellow workers.[148] They had been expelled from Rome, along with the rest of the Jews, by the edict of the emperor Claudius, possibly about A.D. 49. The occasion had been riots among the Jews of Rome "at the instigation of Chrestus,"[149] probably a reference to arguments about Christ between Jews and Christians. Because Aquila and Priscilla, like Paul, were tentmakers,[150] the three worked together.

V. 4. Paul followed his usual procedure of declaring this message in the local synagogue. (See the discussion of 17:1–3.)

Vv. 5–8. When Silas and Timothy arrived from the north (cf. 17:14–15), they apparently brought money or goods with them, so that Paul no longer had to work at his trade.[151] Instead he spent his whole time evangelizing in the synagogue. The Messiah, he declared, had appeared in the person of Jesus. This the Jews violently opposed.

For the second time in Acts, Paul departed from the synagogue and went to the Gentiles (see 13:45–46). The strong feeling against the Jews' blasphemy is seen in Paul shaking out his garments (cf. 13:51, where Paul shook the dust from his feet).

At this point Paul went into a house adjoining the synagogue because the owner of the house, Titius Justus, probably a Roman citizen, was a God-worshiper. A great victory was seen here when the leader[152] of the synagogue, Crispus (cf. I Cor. 1:14), became a convert to the gospel. This led to the conversion of his household, and also of "many of the Corinthians."

148. See also Acts 18:26; Romans 16:3–5; I Corinthians 16:19; II Timothy 4:19.

149. The reference is in Suetonius's *Life of Claudius,* 25.4.

150. More broadly the word *skēnopoioi* means "leather-worker," and applied to more than tentmaking. Paul's homeland, Cilicia, was famous for the manufacture of a cloth made from goat's hair, called *cilicium.*

151. Compare II Corinthians 11:8; Philippians 4:15.

152. An *archisynagōgos* was a person in charge of the building and the conduct of the services. Sometimes there were several in a synagogue (see Mark 5:22; Acts 13:15).

Vv. 9–11. Paul may have been concerned about the ferocity of the Jewish opposition (especially following the conversion of Crispus). In addition, he seemed to have had some apprehension about ministering in Corinth initially (see I Cor. 2:3). Thus the Lord appeared during the night and spoke to Paul through a vision, giving him pointed instructions: "Do not be afraid any longer, but go on speaking and do not be silent"; and assurance of His protection, "for I am with you. . . ." In the dark valley the Shepherd goes before and provides protection for His own (Ps. 23:4).

Paul's stay in Corinth (eighteen months) was longer than his stay in any other place of ministry except Ephesus (Acts 19:10).

Vv. 12–17. Gallio was the brother of the noted Stoic philosopher Seneca, who was also tutor to Nero Caesar. Archaeologists, in discovering the famous inscription at Delphi in Greece,[153] have provided a fixed chronological point for dating Paul's career. Gallio seems to have been proconsul of Achaia during A.D. 51–52. Of him Seneca said, "No mortal is so pleasant to any one person as Gallio is to everybody."

The Jews seized Paul, brought him before the *bēma* (cf. 12:21) and charged him with advocating a religion "contrary to the law." While they disagreed with Paul's interpretation of Judaism (see vv. 5–6), Gallio quickly saw it was an internal squabble, not a violation of Roman law. Thus he dismissed the case. His decision was important for the immediate future of the gospel, for it bestowed the same protection which had been accorded Judaism. At this the incensed Jews beat Sosthenes, the successor to Crispus as ruler of the synagogue in Corinth. Sosthenes may have become a Christian (cf. I Cor. 1:1), but we cannot be sure.

i. Ephesus (18:18–22)

V. 18. Paul, along with Priscilla and Aquila, took ship for Syria, probably intending to return to Antioch or to go south toward Jerusalem. While the "he" is ambiguous, "perhaps the run of the sentence suggests Paul rather than Aquila"[154] as the antecedent. The vow mentioned would probably have been a

---

153. See Adolph Deissmann, *Paul* (New York: Harper & Row, 1957), pp. 261ff.
154. Lake and Cadbury, *Beginnings*, IV, 229.

short-term Nazarite vow (cf. Num. 6), the period ending with
the cutting of the hair. While nothing is known of the circumstances, see Acts 21:23–24 for another example. Paul felt quite
at liberty in such areas (cf. I Cor. 9:19–22).

Vv. 19–22. Paul, Aquila, and Priscilla put into port at Ephesus, then the leading commercial city of the province of Asia.
Paul left Aquila and Priscilla there, where they remained for
several years (see I Cor. 16:9). They later returned to Rome (Rom.
16:3–5).

Once again, Paul entered the synagogue, reasoned with the
Jews, and promised them he would return to them again according to the will of God. On his next visit, he was to spend
more than two years in Ephesus (19:8, 10). Taking ship to Caesarea, Paul went and greeted the church—probably in Jerusalem,
as the phrase "went down to Antioch" implies.[155]

5. The Third Missionary Journey (18:23—21:14)

The areas covered in this journey are similar to those visited
during the second journey, but with some major differences in
the concentration of Paul's efforts. The key province was Asia;
most of his time was spent in Ephesus, with brief visits to Troas
and Miletus. Paul also spent time traveling through Macedonia
and Achaia, spending three months in Greece, probably in Corinth, from where he wrote the letter to the Romans.

a. Galatia (18:23)
Once more Paul traversed the territory covered in his first
and second journeys—the territory of Galatia and Phrygia. He
headed west from Antioch through the famous Cilician Gates
near Tarsus, then finally came to Ephesus (19:1).

b. Apollos at Ephesus (18:24–28)
V. 24. To introduce Apollos, Luke described him in several
ways: a Jew, an Alexandrian by birth, an eloquent (or possibly,
learned) man, and one mighty in the Scriptures.

155. Bruce, *Acts of the Apostles*, p. 350, notes that *katabainō* would not be
used of traveling from Caesarea, a seaport, to Antioch, an inland town. Others
argue for Caesarea, based on the words of Codex Bezae in verse 21: "I must by
all means keep the festival in Jerusalem, but. . . ."

Alexandria was the center of learning in the Greek world, possessing a large library (there the Hebrew Scriptures had been translated into Greek) and a famous university. Philo the Jew lived and wrote there; his works had an influence on the church fathers of the second and third centuries, especially.

Vv. 25–26. Further, Apollos had heard of the Christian message (cf. Acts 9:2 for "the Way") and spoke about Jesus with fervency of spirit.[156] He was a remarkable example of one who could speak, had a message to deliver, and proclaimed that message with spiritual vigor.

Apollos' knowledge apparently was limited to the story of John and his proclamation concerning Jesus. When Priscilla and Aquila heard Apollos speaking in the synagogue, they invited him to their house for further instruction. This may have concerned Christian baptism (cf. Acts 2:38),[157] or the message of the new life of the Spirit in the church.[158] The situation described in Acts 19:1–7 may shed some light on the question.

Vv. 27–28. Apollos apparently accepted and taught the fuller message, for when he desired to go to Achaia (to Corinth, cf. I Cor. 1:12; 3:4–6), the brethren wrote urging the believers to welcome him. Further, Luke recorded, he was a great help to the believers there, which is another proof of his own growth, for shortly before Paul had spent more than eighteen months there, "teaching the Word of God among them" (Acts 18:11). Apollos' message about Jesus was much like what Paul had taught (cf. 17:2–3; 18:5).

c. Paul at Ephesus (19)

This is one of Luke's longest accounts of Paul's work in any one place, and it should be noted that the emphases of the narrative recur in Paul's letter to Ephesus. These emphases are principally four: (1) the presence of the Holy Spirit (vv. 1–7); (2) the conflict with the synagogue, and the Jewish-Gentile issue (vv.

156. The word translated "fervent" is zeōn, meaning "boiling" or "bubbling over." We might say today "enthusiastic" (as we do not retain the original meaning). A similar phrase occurs in Romans 12:11.

157. Bruce, *The Book of Acts*, pp. 381–382.

158. Rackham, *Acts of the Apostles*, p. 343.

8–10); (3) the presence of the demonic (vv. 11–20); and (4) the worship of Artemis (vv. 21–41)[159]

(1) The presence of the Holy Spirit (vv. 1–3). After Apollos had left Ephesus for Corinth, Paul came across the higher ground from Galatia, arriving in Ephesus for what proved to be a long stay (see 18:23). He found some disciples, twelve men (v. 7). Who were they—disciples of the teacher Apollos? The emphasis on "John's baptism" in 18:25 and 19:3 may suggest that. Were they Christians? The usage of "disciples" in Acts may suggest that as its normal sense.

The situation here may be compared with that of the Samaritans who believed through Philip's preaching, but did not receive the Holy Spirit until Peter and John laid their hands upon them (Acts 8:12, 14–17). It is noteworthy that in Acts the Holy Spirit was always imparted to *groups of people* in the presence of an apostle (see chaps. 2, 8, 10, 19).

Paul's question to these men (v. 2) is rightly rendered, "Did you receive the Holy Spirit when you believed?" as a study of the Greek tenses will show.[160] Phrased differently, it means, "Did you receive the Holy Spirit at the time you trusted in Christ?" In the New Testament letters it is assumed that the two belong together (cf. Rom. 8:9; I Cor. 6:19–20; Gal. 4:6; Eph. 1:13–14). What did these men mean by their reply, then? Possibly they had not heard about the Holy Spirit being imparted to anyone. Recall, again, that John the Baptist had only predicted the coming of the Spirit; he had not imparted the Spirit (cf. Acts 1:5; 11:16). With this statement may be compared the words of John 7:39; "for the Spirit was not yet given."

Vv. 4–7. These men received Christian baptism, and when Paul laid his hands on them they received the Holy Spirit. In evidence of this they spoke in tongues and prophesied.

This is the final passage (one of four) in Acts in which groups of people received the Holy Spirit. Notice that the only elements

159. For (1) See Ephesians 1:13–14; 2:18, 22; 3:5, 16: 4:4, 30; 5:18; 6:17–18; (2) see Ephesians 2:11–22; 3:6; (3) see Ephesians 6:10–20; and (4) Ephesians 2:19–20.

160. The verb is aorist (*elabete*) and so is the participle (*pisteusantes*). The action of an aorist participle is normally simultaneous with, sometimes antecedent to, that of the verb.

that retain the same order are repentance/faith and reception of the Spirit. Elements such as baptism with water and speaking in tongues are not always in the same relation to the others; in one case (e.g., the Samaritans), speaking in tongues is not mentioned. What are the implications? First, the Holy Spirit is sovereign in His working—"as He wills" (I Cor. 12:11). Second, the sign of God's acceptance of all kinds of people—Jews, Samaritans, Gentiles—is the gift of the Spirit (I Cor. 12:13). Third, the importance of acknowledging Jesus as Lord is paramount in receiving the Holy Spirit.

(2) The conflict with the synagogue (vv. 8–9). Paul returned to the synagogue in Ephesus (cf. 18:19–21), carrying on his dialogue concerning the kingdom of God. Once more Jewish opposition arose, and, as before, Paul withdrew, reasoning with the disciples in the school of Tyrannus, just as he had done in the house of Titius Justus in Corinth (18:7). An interesting, and not improbable, addition in Codex Bezae is that Paul taught "from the fifth to the tenth hour" (i.e., from 11:00 A.M. to 4:00 P.M.), a time when the public life of the city was largely suspended.[161]

V. 10. During this period the word of the Lord spread throughout the province of Asia, as both Jews and Greeks were being evangelized. This was a crucial period in Paul's life. Many churches were begun, not only in Colossae, Laodicea, and Hierapolis (Col. 4:13), but possibly the others mentioned in the Apocalypse as well (Rev. 1:11). Also, Paul suffered much during these years (see I Cor. 15:32; 16:9; II Cor. 1:8–11); some scholars suppose he experienced imprisonments here as well (cf. II Cor. 11:23).

(3) The presence of the demonic. Ephesus was a center of magic and exorcism, and books containing incantations were called Ephesian letters. In addition, the Jews had a prominent role in magical practices in the ancient world. The use of the name of Jesus in exorcisms was known to the Jews, although the rabbis objected to it as to a pagan practice.

---

161. Lake and Cadbury, Beginnings, IV, 239, add: "At 1 P.M. there were probably more people sound asleep than at 1 A.M., this five-hour period being devoted to the mid-day meal and the siesta."

Vv. 11–12. God showed his power in this center by working in "extraordinary" ways by the hands of Paul. The word used here occurs also in Acts 28:2, indicating something of unusual character. Sweatcloths and aprons that Paul had worn in his leatherworking trade became instruments of healing, even as the tassels of Jesus' garment (Mark 5:27; 6:56) and Peter's shadow (5:15) had brought healing to sick persons.

Vv. 13–16. Some Jewish exorcists attempted to imitate Paul's deeds, using the name of Jesus. An example of this sort of thing is found in the noted Paris Magical Papyrus: "I adjure thee by Jesus the God of the Hebrews," an expression attributed to a pagan writer by Deissmann.[162] Rather than subduing the evil spirit, this formula enraged him, for he recognized these exorcists as fraudulent persons, and he attacked and wounded them, forcing them to flee from the house.

Vv. 17–20. The news of this incident spread quickly, and as a result a great awe fell upon the people of Ephesus. They had seen a mighty work of God, through the gospel, in their midst, and a disarming of the powers of evil. In addition, Luke added, many came to confess their former practices[163] and others to burn their books (actually, scrolls) of magical spells, a way of repudiating their former way of life and thought. Since the unit of money is not mentioned in the Greek text, one can only surmise what the value of the scrolls may have been.[164]

(4) The worship of Artemis (vv. 21–22). At the end of this lengthy period, Paul was led by the Spirit to go next to Jerusalem (after a visit to Macedonia and Achaia, cf. 20:1–2) and then on to Rome. This same planning is indicated a little later in his letter to the Romans (see Rom. 15:22–29). To prepare the way for his visit, he sent Timothy and a man named Erastus into Macedonia.

Vv. 23–28. This is Luke's account of the speech of the Ephesian Demetrius, a silversmith engaged in the manufacture of

162. Deissmann, Light, p. 260.
163. Literally, "magic spells," which, when confessed, would be rendered powerless.
164. If the unit was the Greek drachmē (equivalent to the denarius), that equaled a day's wage for a laborer. Thus, in buying power, it would total 50,000 days' wages.

silver shrines which worshipers of the goddess Artemis would purchase and then dedicate to her in the famous temple outside the city.[165] This was the source of no little profit (cf. Acts 16:16) for the guild of craftsmen.

The thrust of Demetrius' words was that Paul was persuading people that "gods made with hands" (idols) were nonentities, and that this idea, if believed, would result in the temple of the great goddess falling into worthlessness. This strong religious plea was intended to buttress his concern "that this trade of ours fall into disrepute"! His words concerning the extent of her worship—"Asia and the world"—were not wholly an exaggeration, as is shown by archaelogical evidence; at least thirty-three places are mentioned as sites of that devotion.[166] This passionate speech brought an equally passionate response from his hearers, and they began sounding the praises of the goddess.

Vv. 29–31. The crowd rushed into the great theater of Ephesus, a structure that is well-preserved and used for various functions today. Its capacity is about twenty-five thousand persons. Two of Paul's fellow workers—Gaius of Derbe and Aristarchus of Thessalonica (see 20:4)—were dragged into the theater, and when Paul wanted to enter he was restrained by the disciples. Even some of the leading men (Asiarchs) of the cities of Asia warned him not to enter. This datum is important in showing that Christianity was not the object of government opposition at this point in history.

Vv. 32–34. Amid the confusion—the majority of people did not know why the crowd had gathered—the Jews put forward a certain Alexander, at which the crowd may have assumed (the verb is not clear here; it usually means "instructed" in the LXX) he was the cause of the problem. But he was recognized to be a Jew; the shouting began again—for about two hours!

Vv. 35–41. This paragraph provides one of the finest New Testament illustrations of a government official in action. The

165. The Temple of Artemis, a goddess of great antiquity, whose worship as the Great Mother of Asia goes back to earliest time, was regarded as one of the seven wonders of the ancient world. It was built on what was then the seashore, about one and one-half miles outside the city.

166. See Lake and Cadbury, *Beginnings,* IV, 247; Bruce, *Acts of the Apostles,* p. 364.

"townclerk" (*grammateus*) was the secretary, or the chief executive officer, of the city, responsible for issuing the decrees of the *dēmos*, or city government. He, though an Ephesian, was in close touch with the Roman representatives in the province.[167] His words, reminding the Ephesians of their rank as "guardian of the temple" of Artemis and of her image which Jupiter/Zeus had cast down to earth,[168] and also vindicating the accused from any charges of being temple-robbers or blasphemers of Artemis, served to quiet the crowd. He also warned them of the danger of reprisals by the Roman authorities if any riot occurred. They had the Roman courts and their own regular town meetings (*ekklēsia*) in which things could be settled. Let problems be handled according to protocol. And with these words he dismissed the gathering.

d. Macedonia and Greece (20:1–6)

Vv. 1–2. Paul left Ephesus following this incident, although Luke did not give any reason for his departure. According to II Corinthians 2:12–13 and 7:5–7, Paul was concerned about the outcome of Titus' mission to Corinth, and went up through Troas, preaching as he went, until he met Titus in Macedonia. The report gave Paul great comfort and joy. Working his way to the south, Paul came to Greece[169] (probably referring to Corinth) and spent three months there.

Vv. 3–6. Paul's plan to sail from Corinth (Cenchrea) to Syria was changed when he heard of a plot against him. Proceeding overland, he went through Macedonia instead, accompanied by representatives of churches from various provinces: Sopater, Aristarchus, and Secundus from Macedonia; Gaius[170] and Timo-

167. See A. H. M. Jones, *The Greek City* (Oxford: Clarendon Press, 1940), pp. 238–239.

168. The word *diepotes* refers to an object fallen from the sky, and is usually considered to mean a meteorite. This was also true of the stone symbolizing the Great Mother of Asia, brought to Rome from Pessinus.

169. This is the only occurrence of the name *Greece (Hellas)* in the New Testament. In Acts 18:12, Luke had referred to the Roman name *Achaia*, in connection with Gallio's proconsulship. Generally, Luke preferred popular names, Paul provincial names, as in I Corinthians 16:1, 5, 15, 19.

170. Codex Bezae says Gaius was from Doberus (in Macedonia), rather than Derbe (in Galatia). In that case Timothy would have been the lone representative from Galatia.

thy from Galatia; and Tychicus and Trophimus from Asia. They, no doubt, were accompanying Paul as he took the collection to Jerusalem (cf. I Cor. 16:1–4; II Cor. 2–9; Rom. 15:25–27).

Sailing from Philippi (Neapolis), following the time of the spring festival of unleavened bread, Paul arrived five days later (the winds made this journey considerably longer than the one described in 16:11). Luke had rejoined the party; thus the details in the story are more vivid (than, for example, in 20:1–3).

e. Troas (20:7–12)

V. 7. Bruce calls this data "the earliest unambiguous evidence we have for the Christian practice of gathering together for worship on that day."[171] Yet this may not exclude daily celebration of the "breaking of bread," according to Haenchen,[172] as the early Christians in Jerusalem may have done (cf. Acts 2:42, 46). Whether the meeting convened on Saturday evening (counting in the Jewish manner that the new day began at sunset), or whether it was on Sunday (counting in the Roman manner that the new day began at midnight) is not clear.

Vv. 8–12. The story of the fatal fall of Eutychus, and his restoration to life by Paul's ministration, is told simply, without any great detail. Luke the physician (who was present) says Eutychus "was picked up dead"; Paul embraced the body (cf. I Kings 17:21; II Kings 4:34–35) and restored his life. Calmly following this by more eating and conversation, Paul then departed for points south.

f. Miletus (20:13–38)

Vv. 13–16. Details about the approach to Miletus were given in matter-of-fact fashion, without explaining why Paul traveled from Troas to Assos by land, and the rest of the way by sea. Further, we learn here that Paul decided to bypass Ephesus to be in Jerusalem for the festival of Pentecost.

Vv. 17–21. Summoning the elders of the church in Ephesus to him at Miletus, Paul recalled the work he had done among them. This is the only example Luke has given of a speech of

171. Bruce, *The Book of Acts*, pp. 407–408; he cites Oscar Cullmann, *Early Christian Worship*, in support.
172. Haenchen, *Acts of the Apostles*, p. 584.

Paul to believers; the others were to adherents of the synagogues (e.g., 13:16–41) and to pagan audiences (e.g., 14:15–17; 17:22–31). Further, Paul seems to have had an apologetic motive in mind, for the speech appears to defend his ministry against disruptive elements in Asia (cf. I Cor. 16:9b; and Acts 20:29–31, where he anticipated danger).

Notice the brief descriptions of the manner and content of Paul's ministry in Ephesus, which, by their very candidness, shed a great light about the nature of early Christianity. First, it was *public* (cf. 18:28, of Apollos' preaching); a feature descriptive of Paul's work in the synagogue and the school of Tyrannus. Second, it was also *in the homes* of the people (cf. 2:46, of the practice of the new church in Jerusalem). Third, to all people (both Jews and Greeks) Paul's basic message was the same: repentance toward God and faith in Christ. These are the twin emphases of the gospel: turning from sin to the Savior.

Vv. 22–27. Paul turned to some remarks about his future. He felt it "his bounden duty" (to borrow a phrase from the Book of Common Prayer) to go on to Jerusalem, knowing only that the Holy Spirit was testifying to dangers ahead. Yet this did not dissuade Paul. "Self-preservation was not a motive highly esteemed" by him[173]—he would press on to fulfill what he believed to be the course marked out for him by Christ, that is, the proclamation of the good news.

A theological point of some importance emerges here, especially in view of some extremist distinctions between major themes in the New Testament. In verse 24, Paul referred to proclaiming "the gospel of the grace of God," and in verse 25, he recalled his "preaching the kingdom." No difference is suggested. Jesus prepared His apostles for their ministry by speaking during the final forty days "of the things concerning the kingdom of God" (Acts 1:3); and Paul taught "concerning the Lord Jesus Christ" in proclaiming "the kingdom of God" (28:31), showing that the two are really one. The good news about Jesus (the gospel) is that the kingdom of God has come and will also be revealed in full glory at the second advent of our Lord.

Paul expressed what he believed would be his final farewell

173. Bruce, *The Book of Acts*, p. 414.

to the elders (v. 25), affirming that he had declared "the whole purpose of God" for them (cf. v. 20).

Vv. 28–35. A charge was laid upon the leaders of the church (here they are called "overseers" [bishops]; notice "elders" in v. 17 above). The Holy Spirit had gifted them for their ministry. They were to "shepherd" (tend) the church under their care, for it was really God's church, and He had purchased it at a great cost, by the blood of His Son (cf. Eph. 1:7, 14; 5:25; I Peter 1:18–19; Rev. 5:9–10).[174]

Even as the Lord God of Israel was a Shepherd to Israel (Isa. 40:11), while being Ruler over them (Isa. 40:10), and as Christ is both Lord and Shepherd to His own, so the human leaders of the church were to tend the flock of God. This theme is common in the New Testament (see, e.g., Eph. 4:11, "pastors," synonymous with "shepherd"; John 21:15–17; I Peter 5:1–4).

Second, the leaders were to be alert against the rise of false teachers ("savage wolves") who would attempt to destroy the flock. Even from within the church would trouble arise, leading to the danger of divisions. Jesus had warned His disciples of this danger (see Matt. 7:15–20; 24:24); such false teachers would be hirelings who would not be concerned about the sheep (John 10:13). As years passed this danger became a reality (see especially I Tim. 4:1–6; 6:3–5, written to Timothy at Ephesus; and the epistles of II Peter, I and II John, and Jude).

Third, Paul commended these leaders to God and to the word of His grace. To "commend" (in this instance) means "to entrust" (cf. II Tim. 1:12, 14); Paul himself had been commended or committed to the grace of God by the church at Antioch (Acts 14:26; 15:40). What is "the word of His grace"? Rackham[175] has put it pointedly: "This message of the free bounty of God is the word

174. The words translated "with His own blood" might be rendered "with the blood of His own" (*dia tou haimatos tou idiou*), meaning "His own [Son]." The textual history of the verse is a long one, and has inspired some heated theological arguments. In some manuscripts, instead of "the church of God" we read "the church of the Lord," the latter being an attempt to relate better to the final phrase, "with His own blood," that is, "the Lord's (Christ's) blood."

175. Rackham, *Acts of the Apostles*, p. 395.

which has the greatest effect on the heart of man, and so it is *able to build up* the church" (italics his).

Finally, Paul appealed to his own example as a model for the elders (vv. 33–35). He had labored hard among the Ephesians to meet his material needs, and the needs of those who accompanied him. This was an illustration of the gospel in action. The good news includes the bodies as well as the souls of people, and that was what the Lord Jesus meant by His teaching recorded here.[176]

Vv. 36–38. There is much tenderness in Luke's description of Paul kneeling down and praying aloud for these brothers in the faith, and their response is equally moving: with loud weeping, expressive of their sorrow, they fell on his neck and kissed him repeatedly.[177] Reluctant to let him depart, these leaders accompanied Paul to the ship, which was to take him to Caesarea,[178] from where he would travel to Jerusalem.

g. *Tyre (21:1–6)*

Vv. 1–3. Leaving Miletus, the ship "ran a straight course" to Cos, then to Rhodes, and finally to Patara. The first two places are islands, the last a seaport on the south coast of Lycia. Here the group boarded a different ship for the voyage to Phoenicia.[179]

During the summer season the prevailing winds were northwesterly. Thus a continuous voyage, within a period of five days, was quite possible in the southerly and eastern direction.

The ship sailed past Cyprus (sighted on the port side), making for Tyre, there to unload the cargo. St. Chrysostom says this

---

176. While these words of Jesus (v.35) are not found in the Gospels, they reflect the spirit of many of His sayings, and this was a principle also common to Judaism and to Greek ethics. See Lake and Cadbury, *Beginnings*, IV, 264. There is an excellent discussion of this whole speech, as well as definitive comments on the office of presbyter/bishop in Rackham, *Acts of the Apostles*, pp. 382–387, as well as verse-by-verse comments.

177. The imperfect tense, *katephiloun:* "they kept on kissing."

178. The missionaries may have gone by ship only as far as Ptolemais, then journeyed by road to Caesarea, a distance of nearly forty miles.

179. Codex Bezae adds the words "and Myra" after Patara, indicating the change in ship took place there. Myra was the essential port in Mediterranean shipping going to Syria and Egypt.

voyage (of about four hundred miles) took five days, indicating a continuous voyage.

Vv. 4–6. During the seven-day wait at Tyre,[180] while the ship unloaded its cargo, Paul visited the disciples, probably converts from the days following Stephen's death (cf. 11:19). These people warned Paul about the danger awaiting him in Jerusalem, exhibiting a genuine spiritual concern[181] for his welfare. Why did Paul not heed this warning? The answer may lie in Luke's previous narrative (see 20:22–23), where Paul testified to the same kind of inward impression. But the concern in both cases was for Paul's physical safety. He was not primarily concerned about that, but about fulfilling his mission (see also 21:10–14). Another touching farewell followed, and Paul and his company boarded ship for Ptolemais.

h. Caesarea (21:7–14)

Vv. 7–9. From Tyre the party sailed to Ptolemais, and after staying a day with the brethren there, proceeded on to Caesarea. These people, as those at Tyre (vv. 4–5), may have been converts of the disciples who scattered from Jerusalem. Philip the evangelist (cf. Acts 8:12, 35, 40) was last described as coming to Caesarea following an extensive preaching ministry in Samaria and Judea. Luke notes here that he was "one of the seven" (cf. 6:3, 5), probably to distinguish him from Philip the apostle (1:13). Like Stephen, Philip was known as a Hellenist, and an ardent proclaimer of the message concerning Jesus. In addition, his four daughters possessed the gift of prophecy, a gift also known in the church at Corinth (I Cor. 11:5).

Vv. 10–12. Not only Philip, but Agabus also, reappears in this passage (cf. Acts 11:27–28). Coming to Caesarea from Judea, Agabus acted out Paul's impending fate if he proceeded to Jerusalem.[182] The apostle, he warned, would be bound and deliv-

---

180. Compare 20:6 regarding Troas, where the missionaries stayed seven days.

181. The phrase "through the Spirit" (*dia tou pneumatos*) is ambiguous, but probably refers to a divinely-inspired utterance or prophecy.

182. Often in the Old Testament the prophets acted out their predictions, sometimes in a very graphic manner, for example, Isaiah 20:4; Jeremiah 13:11; Ezekiel 4:1–13.

ered over to the Gentiles. Once again (see v. 4) the warning given by the Holy Spirit was about danger awaiting Paul; it was not a prohibition against going to Jerusalem.

Vv. 13–14. Paul was well aware of danger. By now he was a veteran in suffering for Christ. His continued affirmation of being ready to die for his Lord persuaded his friends to appeal to the will of God for him. Had he not, shortly before this, written Romans 8:28–39?

V. Imprisonment: The Gospel in Jerusalem, Caesarea, and Rome (21:15—28:31)

Striking it is indeed that Luke, in writing the story of the missionary outreach of the early church, should devote about one-fourth of his narrative to Paul's imprisonment in Jerusalem, Caesarea, and Rome.[183] The time period was proportionately short, being something more than four years, as compared with more than twenty-five years covered in the rest of Acts. Yet it was an important conclusion to the story, for by these means the gospel reached Rome, Paul was delivered from many a danger, and the story of the first generation of Christianity was brought to a stirring climax.[184]

A. Paul Taken Prisoner in Jerusalem (21:15–36)

As noted earlier, Paul felt he must go to Jerusalem to deliver the collection of funds from the churches of Galatia, Macedonia, Achaia, and Asia. This had not only been a request from the Jerusalem leadership (cf. Gal. 2:10), but also was a factor in showing a unity of spirit and a genuine concern of Christian brothers for one another. So Paul must have viewed it (cf. Rom. 15:25–27).

Luke made no reference to the collection at this point, nor is it clearly mentioned anywhere in Acts, except for Paul's words before Felix, "I came to bring alms to my nation and to present offerings" (24:17). Yet to Paul it was a great moment (see especially II Cor. 8–9).

---

183. Notice in Luke's Gospel the amount of space given to the narrative of the Passion Week (18:31—24:49). In Mark's Gospel about three-eighths is devoted to this period.

184. Rackham, *Acts of the Apostles*, pp. 403–405, gives several reasons for the extended description: the personal factor—Luke's recollection of Paul's experiences during this period; the artistic factor—a parallel to the passion of Christ, and to the sufferings of Peter (see Acts 2–8); and the practical factor—to give a record of Paul's defence before both Jews and Romans.

Vv. 15–16. Somewhere between Caesarea and Jerusalem the party lodged with "a disciple of long standing," Mnason of Cyprus. Was he possibly one of Luke's informants about some of the early history of the gospel in that area? Ramsay[185] suggests that he, like Lydia and others in the story, was a source for certain episodes (the stories of Aeneas and Dorcas) in Luke's narrative.

Vv. 17–19. Paul and his group were received gladly by the brethren—quite a contrast with his first visit (see 9:26)! The official reception occurred the following day, before James and all the elders. No mention is made of the apostles (see 15:4, 22); thus we may assume they were not present in Jerusalem. Paul talked about his work among the Gentiles, and presented the money collected from the churches.

Vv. 20–26. These two things caused the leaders to glorify God, for they were thankful for both the conversions and the practical expression of concern for the needy in Jerusalem.

Yet there was a disturbing factor. Among the "many thousands" (myriades, lit., "ten thousands") of believing Jews, "all zealous for the Law" (even as Paul himself had been, Gal. 1:14, and as "the Pharisees who had believed," Acts 15:5) a rumor concerning Paul had been circulated. It had been reported that he had been teaching the Jews of the Dispersion to forsake loyalty to the law of Moses—not to circumcise their children or to follow the Jewish ethic (cf. Acts 6:14).

While we have no evidence the rumor was true, it posed a serious problem. But a suggestion was made to disprove it. If Paul would be willing to join four men who had undertaken a seven-day Nazarite vow, pay their expenses at the temple, and submit to a purificatory rite, he would demonstrate his conformity to the law and the customs of Israel.[186]

The leaders assured Paul they were not wishing to impose any requirements upon the Gentile believers; the Jerusalem council had already decided that issue (15:22–29). Thus Paul

185. Ramsay, Recent Discovery, p. 309. He also mentions Sergius Paulus and Simon of Samaria as "full of historic significance."

186. On the Nazarite vow, see Numbers 6:13–20. It included the offering of various sacrifices and shaving one's head.

followed the proposed action. This seems to have been quite in keeping with his principle stated in I Corinthians 9:19–22.

Vv. 27–30. However, the plan did not go well, for some Asian Jews, who had arrived in Jerusalem for the festival of Pentecost, attempted to carry out a plot against Paul (cf. 20:19). Supposing he had taken a Gentile (Trophimus the Ephesian) into the court of Israel—an area for Jewish men only—these Asian Jews raised a cry against Paul.[187] Laying violent hands upon him, they dragged him out of the temple (i.e., the sanctuary). The temple police at once closed the gates leading into the sanctuary to safeguard the holy place.

Vv. 31–32. Happily for Paul, word spread quickly to the Roman commander in Jerusalem that a riot was under way. The commander and his troops, stationed in the Fortress of Antonia, at the northwest corner of the temple area, responded at once. With at least two hundred soldiers,[188] the Roman rushed down the steps into the court of the Gentiles, bringing to a temporary halt the beating of Paul.

Vv. 33–36. Putting Paul under formal arrest by chaining him to two soldiers, the captain (later identified by name, Claudius Lysias, 23:26), attempted to discover the prisoner's crime. The cries from the mob brought no clear answer, only confusion. Thus the commander ordered that Paul be brought into the fortress for interrogation. So violent was the crowd that the soldiers had to carry Paul bodily to protect him, while the cry echoed, "Away with him!" More than twenty-five years earlier that same cry had echoed from Pilate's judgment hall (Luke 23:18; John 19:15).

B. Paul's Defense before the Jews (21:37—22:29)

At this point began a series of interrogations, trials, and speeches, the record of which extends through chapter 26. There are similarities in the various episodes, yet certain distinctive

187. The court of the Gentiles was the only area in the temple precincts allowed to Gentiles. See comments on Acts 3:1–3 for details.

188. Luke referred to "centurions" (v. 32), each responsible for 100 men; thus 200 would be the minimum number implied.

features appear as well. One element is the differing emphases directed to different audiences. For example, when addressing Roman officials, Paul stressed his local (Tarsian) background and his Roman citizenship; when addressing Jews, he stressed his Jewish background, training, and loyalty. The larger part of the narrative is given over to Paul's dealings with Roman personnel—this probably was Luke's way of emphasizing that the Roman government had laid no official sanction against the gospel and its emissaries. The words of Agrippa to Festus, which conclude this entire section, are significant: "This man might have been set free if he had not appealed to Caesar" (26:32).

Vv. 37–39. When Paul asked permission of the captain to speak to him, the officer was surprised that his prisoner could speak Greek. As verse 38 shows, the captain had mistaken Paul for an Egyptian, who three years before had led an insurrection against Rome, promising his four thousand followers that God would aid their course.[189] Since the man had escaped, Claudius Lysias wondered if he had apprehended this man in the person of Paul. The companions of the rebel had been known as "the Assassins" (the *sicarii*, lit., "the dagger men"), avowed enemies of the Roman government and of Jews sympathetic to it.

Paul's reply, deadly serious, had also a wry note of humor in it. Can we visualize, even in present-day Jerusalem, a Jew being mistaken for an Egyptian? Paul replied in terse language: "I am a man . . . a Jew . . . a citizen of Tarsus."[190] He did not mention his Roman citizenship, and the claim to his Tarsian citizenship made little impression on the captain. Paul requested and received permission to address the people gathered in the court below.

V. 40. Gaining the attention of the people by a motion of the hand (cf. 12:17; 13:16; 19:33), Paul addressed them in the vernacular of Palestine, the Aramaic tongue (the language of Syria, and the common speech of much of the Near East).

189. For a description of this rebel, see Josephus, *Antiquities* 20. 8.6 and *Jewish War* 2. 13.4–5. Josephus claimed the man had thirty thousand followers.

190. Lake and Cadbury, *Beginnings*, IV, 278, state that as a "Jew" Paul claimed a right to be in the temple, and as a Diaspora Jew he explained his acquaintance with Greeks.

Vv. 1–4. Having quieted the crowd, Paul first laid heavy emphasis on his Jewish background. He began much as he did in 21:39 (above), but added data concerning his training under the famous Rabban Gamaliel in Jerusalem,[191] and his zeal for God (a kind of zeal possessed by his hearers also), even to the extent of persecuting "this Way" (i.e., "the church," I Cor. 15:9; Gal. 1:13).

A crucial literary characteristic is the triad, "born . . . brought up . . . educated" (v. 3). It has been argued in recent years that the second element shows that Paul was reared from a very young age in Jerusalem, rather than growing up to adolescence or young manhood in Tarsus.[192]

Vv. 5–16. This is the second account of Paul's conversion in Acts (see the comments about 9:1–16). Some details that were not mentioned in the earlier passage are added. First, the bright light shone upon Paul "about noontime" (v. 6). Second, only here does Jesus identify Himself as "Jesus the Nazarene" (v. 8). Third, Paul's companions did not hear the voice of Jesus (contrast 9:7). This probably means they did not hear with understanding (cf. John 12:29–30), or it may refer to two different voices, Paul's in 9:7, and Jesus' in 22:8. Fourth, Ananias is described as a devout Jew, highly respected by the Jews of Damascus (v. 12), whereas in 9:10 Luke calls him "a certain disciple." Fifth, Ananias addressed Paul as "brother," and referred to "the God of our fathers" (vv. 13–14). All these data are intended to appeal to the Jewish audience listening to Paul's words. Finally, Ananias exhorted Paul to rise from his bed, "and be baptized, and wash away your sins, calling on His name" (v. 16). There are two important precedents for this kind of response: the preaching of John the Baptist (see Luke 3:3); and the preaching of Peter (see Acts 2:38). This was, first, a call to repentance of sin; and God would forgive such (cf. Acts 3:19). Second, "calling on His name" may refer to the invocation of

191. On Gamaliel, see the comments about Acts 5:34.
192. Especially see W. C. van Unnik, *Tarsus or Jerusalem: the City of Paul's Youth* (London: Epworth, 1962), *passim*. Similar words describe Moses in Acts 7:20–22: "born . . . nurtured . . . educated" (the same three Greek words being used).

divine blessing, and baptism "in the name of Jesus" (cf. Acts 2:38; 10:48).

Vv. 17–21. Paul recounted his commission to go to the Gentiles. Upon his return to Jerusalem after his conversion (cf. 9:26), he was praying in the temple and received a vision. The Lord appeared to him, telling him to leave Jerusalem quickly, for the Jews would not receive his witness concerning Jesus (cf. 9:29). Paul remonstrated, arguing that the drastic change in him, from persecutor to proclaimer of the good news, would amply qualify him for the task. But the Lord's words were final: Paul was to go to the Gentiles (cf. 9:30). Thus began his ministry as apostle to the nations.

Vv. 22–29. That last word did it! When the crowd heard "Gentiles," they exploded in rage. Once again they cried for Paul's death, accompanying their words with physical acts of disgust. The Jews did not consider it wrong to convert Gentiles (cf. Matt. 23:15), but they suspected Paul's motives as well as his message. At this point the Roman captain ordered Paul brought inside the fortress, for safety. Also, he determined he must find out the truth about the prisoner. Why was Paul so ardently hated by his countrymen? Thus the captain ordered Paul to be scourged.

Now Paul claimed the protection of the law guaranteed to Roman citizens. Legally, they were protected from beatings, scourgings, and crucifixion. This claim came as a shock to both the centurion present, and to Claudius Lysias, for, up to this point, Paul had been regarded as a kind of revolutionary character.

The captain asserted that he had paid a great sum of money to obtain his citizenship, a practice common in the reign of Claudius Caesar. Bruce renders the reading of Codex Bezae here, "It cost me a huge sum; it seems to have become cheap nowadays."[193] But Paul replied that he was freeborn! (How his father had obtained the citizenship we we do not know.) So the problem remained unsolved: Claudius Lysias was worried as to the propriety of holding the prisoner in chains.

193. Bruce, *Acts of the Apostles*, p. 407.

C. Paul's Defense before the Sanhedrin (22:30—23:10)

V. 30. The decision was made to bring Paul before the high Jewish court, the Sanhedrin. Possibly it could determine whether the prisoner was guilty of any capital crime.

V. 1. Standing before the court, Paul looked with "a peculiar fixed look" (Hobart).[194] Then he startled its members with his claim to have lived "with a perfectly good conscience before God up to this day." Before his conversion he had zealously persecuted the church, even voting the death sentence against people (26:10). After his conversion he was a turncoat, one who had turned against the religion of his fathers, in the eyes of his fellow Jews. Yet here and in other places he affirmed he had no consciousness of wrongdoing against God (Acts 26:9; Phil. 3:6, "found blameless").[195]

Vv. 2–3. Paul's bold affirmation, claiming that he was acceptable in God's sight (not on his own merit, but because God is always a God of mercy), and that God alone was his judge (cf. I Cor. 4:4), was not taken lightly by Ananias, the high priest and head of the Sanhedrin. He considered Paul's statement reprehensible and commanded the prisoner to be struck across the mouth.

The apostle's reply, far from being simply an impetuous remark, was prophetic in nature. "God shall smite thee" (KJV) is a malediction taken from Deuteronomy 28:22, a judgment carried out a few years later (A.D. 66) when Ananias was done to death. Calling him a "white-washed wall" described that thin veil covering the man's inner corruption.[196]

194. For some scholars, it is difficult to accept the theory that Paul had poor eyesight. This forceful word (atenizō) was a favorite of Luke. He used it of Paul (13:9; 14:9; 23:1) and of others (1:10; 3:4, 12; 10:4). It is difficult for one afflicted with poor eyesight to look "intently."

195. On the words, "I have lived my life," compare Philippians 1:27, where the same word, with ethical connotations, occurs. The term *conscience* was rarely used in classical Greek and, according to William Fidian Moulton and George Milligan, *The Greek-English Lexicon of the New Testament*, ed. and trans. Joseph Henry Thayer (Grand Rapids: Zondervan, 1962), s.v., suneidēsis, seems to have been "'baptized' by Paul into a new and deeper connotation."

196. The corrupt character of Ananias is noted in Josephus, *Antiquities* 20. 9.2, and by the Babylonian Talmud, from which we learn of his rapacity and greed.

Vv. 4–5. When he was rebuked for using such words against the high priest, Paul confessed he was unaware that the speaker was the head of the council. These words have been variously interpreted. For instance, Paul had not seen the one who had spoken to him; Ananias was not dressed in his official garb and therefore was not recognized as the high priest; or Paul really meant that he could not believe anyone who spoke such words could occupy the office of high priest. Any or all of these possibilities have some credence.

Yet Paul acknowledged the command of the law concerning not speaking evil of a ruler; thus he submitted himself to that very authority he had been accused of ignoring.

Vv. 6–8. Paul shifted his approach. Before Roman rulers he had claimed his citizenship (Acts 16:37; 22:25); now, before Jewish rulers, he claimed his Pharisaic background. He had come from a line of Pharisees and remained one to that day. Nor was Pharisaism incompatible with his Christian faith. He had acknowledged Jesus as the Messiah. Otherwise the tenets of Pharisaism, as we know about them in the early first century, are basic to the Christian faith also,[197] the hope of the resurrection of the dead (as illustrated in Jesus) being central.

This claim had the effect of dividing the Sanhedrin—for Pharisees and Sadducees differed sharply on this issue (cf. Mark 12:18). Luke added, for the sake of his readers, that Sadducees denied both bodily resurrection and the existence of spirit beings. Thus the Pharisees in the Sanhedrin would be more kindly disposed toward Paul for his ideas.

Vv. 9–10. The atmosphere changed. Pharisees began arguing against Sadducees, leaving Paul nearly a spectator. The effect of it all was an adjournment of the session, not by Ananias, but by the Roman commander (cf. 22:29), who feared for Paul's safety. So the prisoner was returned to the barracks to await the next step in the adjudication of his case.

---

197. See, for example, F. C. Grant, *Roman Hellenism in the New Testament* (Edinburgh: Oliver and Boyd, 1957).

D. Paul Taken to Caesarea (23:11–35)

V. 11. This verse is crucial to all that follows, for it assures Paul's arrival in Rome. There were many possible pitfalls in between!

The Lord appeared to Paul during the night, promising him divine protection, and doubtless encouraging him following his harrowing experiences in Jerusalem. This occasion was another like the visions recorded in 16:9, 18:9, 22:17, and one yet to come in 27:23–24.

Vv. 12–15. One of the first dangers threatening Paul's life was a plot laid by certain Jews to kill the prisoner in an ambush. They suggested to the Sanhedrin that a request be sent to the Roman commander to bring Paul out of the barracks for further interrogation. As he would be led along, the zealots would attack and kill the prisoner.

Vv. 16–22. Now occurred another providential circumstance. Paul's nephew, about whom we know nothing else,[198] was in Jerusalem and in a position to overhear the plot being laid. He at once came and reported the facts to Paul.

Calling a centurion, Paul had his nephew taken to the commander to report the plot. The commander showed kindness to the young man, listened to (and believed) his report, and instructed him not to tell anyone that he had notified the commander of what he heard.

Vv. 23–24. The commander ordered two of his centurions to assemble a large company, consisting of 200 soldiers, 70 horseman, and 200 spearmen (or, possibly, men who threw javelins or used slings). Doubtless this sizable group was meant to discourage the assassins from attempting to carry out their plot. Paul was to be put on a mount (a horse or a mule) and delivered safely to the procurator, Felix, in Caesarea, the Roman capital of the province.

Vv. 25–30. An official statement describing the prisoner and the charges against him was written by the commander—now

198. Probably Paul's family had little to do with him following his conversion, but it seems likely his sister and her son had retained good relations with him. The fact that Paul appealed more than once to his ancestry shows that he valued his family background (Acts 23:6; Rom. 11:1; Phil. 3:5).

for the first time named by Luke. Claudius Lysias (named after the emperor Claudius reigning at the time), who acquired his citizenship by purchase (cf. Acts 22:28), here stressed his role in taking care of Paul, no doubt for the benefit of the governor, the "most excellent" Felix.[199]

Lysias related to Felix how he rescued Paul from the mob, "having learned that he was a Roman" (he slightly modified the order of events here); how he had Paul investigated by the council; and how he learned of the plot against Paul's life. In all this he had not discovered any cause why Paul should be imprisoned or put to death; thus he sent Paul to Felix so that the governor might try him.

Vv. 31–35. By night the soldiers took Paul about thirty-five miles to Antipatris (a city northwest of Jerusalem, built by Herod the Great and named after his father, Antipater). Having outdistanced those who had plotted against Paul, the military escort reduced itself to the horsemen who saw the prisoner safely to Caesarea, another twenty-five miles. When Felix learned that Paul was from the Roman province of Cilicia, he ordered Paul held in the governor's headquarters, the palace Herod had built for himself at Caesarea.

Antonius Felix, described by the Roman historian Tacitus as "exercising the power of a king with the mind of a slave" (*Histories* 5.9), was the procurator of Judea from A.D. 52 to 59. His time in office was marked by numerous troubles, especially the rise of the "dagger men" (the *sicarii*), a group already referred to by Luke (see Acts 21:38). They were anti-Roman and moved about the country, murdering their opponents. The fact that the government could not solve this problem was a circumstance that contributed to the onset of the great war in A.D. 66.

E. Paul's Defense before Felix (24)

This is an account of the first of three trials in Roman courtrooms: before Felix, then Festus, and finally Festus and King

---

199. Compare Luke 1:3, where Theophilus was addressed in the same manner; Acts 24:3, of Felix again; and 26:25 of Festus.

Agrippa II. Already Paul had won a verdict of "not guilty" in the opinion of Claudius Lysias.

1. The accusations against Paul (24:1–9)

V. 1. From Jerusalem, after a period of five days, came the accusers: Ananias (the high priest), some of the elders from the council, and an attorney named Tertullus. Nothing is known of the last, yet from the passage we see he was eloquent in his rhetoric, and apprised of both Roman and Jewish law (see the charges in vv. 5–6).

Vv. 2–4. Tertullus's statements concerning Felix in verse 2 are better understood as examples of rhetorical technique than of actual fact. While Felix did suppress disorder by crucifying brigands, his term in office had been anything but peaceful or truly reforming (see commentary about 23:31–35).

Notice the language used by the attorney: "every way . . . everywhere . . . all thankfulness," an example of oratorical speech. Further, Tertullus promised to be brief so as not to weary the governor, and he seems to have kept his word.

Vv. 5–6. The accusations against Paul consisted of three, or possibly four, statements. Those who favor three point to Luke 23:2, where the same root word ("we [have] found") introduces a threefold charge against Jesus. Tertullus said of Paul that he was a "pest," a word meaning "an evil man" or "a plague"; one who stirred up rebellions among the Jews; a ringleader of a troublesome sect, called "the Nazarenes" after the founder, Jesus of Nazareth; and one who tried to desecrate the temple (cf. 21:28). The last led to his arrest.

Vv. 7–9. Verses 7 and 8a do not occur in all Greek manuscripts; they may be an addition by the Western text to explain the role of Claudius Lysias in the affair. He is not put in a very good light by this statement. Further, the expression "by examining him yourself" (v. 8) is then applied to Lysias, not to Paul, as we would usually understand the words, for Felix did call upon Paul to testify next (vv. 10ff.). However, see the words of Felix in verse 22. Following Tertullus's words, the Jews present enthusiastically affirmed that he spoke the truth.

2. Paul's response to his accusers (24:10–21)

Vv. 10–13. Paul responded, although with a considerably shorter introduction than that of Tertullus. He affirmed that he had gone to Jerusalem to worship, not to cause trouble, and denied that in the temple, or the synagogues, or in the city had he stirred up any insurrection. In these very specific words he answered the charges stated in verse 5.

Vv. 14–16. Paul affirmed what was true of his way of life: he was a member of "the Way" (cf. Acts 9:2), worshiped the God of Israel, believed the teaching of the Scriptures, and hoped for the resurrection of both the righteous and the wicked.[200] And, cherishing these things, he had done his best to maintain a clear conscience before God and men (cf. Acts 23:1).

In saying these things, Paul sought to show what he held in common with the very people who accused him. He worshiped the same God ("of our fathers"); he believed the same Scriptures; and he, like they, cherished the hope of the resurrection. This was an orthodox Jewish stance; and in Paul's day Judaism was *religio licita,* a religion not proscribed by the Roman government.

Vv. 17–21. At this point Paul related, briefly, the story of his visit to Jerusalem. He had been present in the temple, with no objection to his presence; everything was in good order as far as the Jews of Jerusalem were concerned. Rather, it was some Jews from Asia who complained—and these very accusers had not even appeared before Felix to press their case. Paul implied that they really had no case at all!

Even those present in the courtroom said nothing. According to Paul, the only charge they could bring was that he believed in the resurrection of the dead. Obviously, such a charge would be self-defeating.

3. Felix postponed a decision (24:22–27)

Vv. 22–23. Felix himself had some insight into the beliefs of the followers of "the Way"; thus he felt it safer to wait for cor-

200. This is the only place in which Paul explicitly affirmed the resurrection of the unjust, but this was a standard Pharisaic teaching, and there is no reason to believe Paul denied it. On the two resurrections see Daniel 12:2; John 5:28–29; Revelation 20:4–6, 12–15.

roborating information from the Roman captain, Claudius Lysias, before rendering his decision. The details of Paul's experiences in Jerusalem could be verified by listening to the captain's testimony.

In the meantime Paul, although a prisoner, was given freedom to visit with friends who would come to him. This treatment of an uncondemned Roman citizen was fitting.

Vv. 24–26. Shortly after this ("some days later") Felix arrived with his third wife, Drusilla, to visit with Paul. Drusilla was a Jewess, one of the daughters of Herod Agrippa I (see Acts 12), and sister to Bernice, who in turn was sister to Herod Agrippa II (cf. Acts 25:13). According to Codex Bezae, it was Drusilla's interest in meeting Paul that led to this visit, and others later.

Paul's message to the pair centered upon the message of righteousness, self-control, and the judgment to come. These remarks were well-aimed, for Drusilla had left her husband—at Felix's persuasion—in order to marry the procurator. The case was not unlike that of Herod Antipas and Herodias, who had been condemned by John (cf. Mark 6:17–18). Thus Felix sent Paul away, for fright gripped him as his conscience testified to his lack of morality.

All the while Paul was held prisoner, Felix was hoping to receive a bribe for his freedom. While Roman law forbade bribery, it was not unknown, and Felix reputedly had been an easy target for monetary gifts.[201]

V. 27. At this point ("after two years") Felix was recalled, and replaced by Porcius Festus. In order to gain favor with the Jews, Felix left Paul in prison, and the case passed into the hands of his successor.

F. Paul's Defense before Festus (25:1–12)

Vv. 1–5. The account is brief in this case, and the trial was virtually a repetition of the hearing before Felix. Festus made a visit to Jerusalem, where the Jewish leaders brought charges against Paul. They requested that the procurator have the prisoner brought to Jerusalem for trial, all the while intending to

201. Haenchen, *Acts of the Apostles*, p. 661.

ambush and kill Paul en route. Festus refused, insisting that the Jews send some leaders to Caesarea, where the hearing would be conducted. Thus the plot was foiled (cf. Acts 23:12–24).

Vv. 6–8. Festus, having returned to Caesarea, assumed his position as the official judge ("he took his seat on the tribunal"; lit., "judgment seat"). The Jews present brought their accusations against Paul (probably similar to those stated by Tertullus in 24:5–6), which, Luke added, "they could not prove." Paul responded by denying wrongdoing in any area: against the Jewish law, the temple, or Caesar. Thus the impasse remained.

Vv. 9–11. As had been the case with Felix, Festus was "wishing to do the Jews a favor" (cf. 24:27). He proposed to Paul that the trial be moved to Jerusalem, with himself presiding.

Paul immediately refused, on the grounds he had done no wrong to the Jews. He may have been afraid that Festus would hand him over to the Sanhedrin. The text, however, tells us Paul was more concerned about his rights as a Roman citizen than his life as such. Thus he said, "I appeal to Caesar." He probably believed justice would be administered impartially by the emperor, Nero.[202]

V. 12. At this Festus was greatly relieved. Now he could dispatch this prisoner to Rome.

G. Paul's Defense before Agrippa (25:13—26:32)

This lengthy account may have been intended by Luke to balance the narrative in 21:37—22:29 (Paul's defense before the Jews), as it gives his defense in the presence of a Roman judge and a Roman-appointed king. In addition, it shows Festus's dilemma about having to send a prisoner to Nero without any established charges against him! Festus hoped Agrippa would be able to find some clue as he listened to Paul.

202. Nero's persecution of Roman Christians is well known, but this did not occur until A.D. 64. During the early years of his reign, Nero had been nearly a model ruler (thanks to the influences of Seneca, the Stoic philosopher, and Burrus, the prefect of the emperor's guard). The years A.D. 54–59 have been called the golden quinquennium.

1. Festus explained the problem to Agrippa (25:13–22)

V. 13. Herod Agrippa II was the great-grandson of Herod the Great. Bernice, his sister, lived with him as a wife. While still a young man Agrippa became ruler of certain territories in Palestine, the areas which had been given to his father (Agrippa I) by the emperor Gaius in A.D. 37. When Nero presented other territory to him in A.D. 56, Herod changed the name of the famous city of Caesarea Philippi to Neronias. When the great war of A.D. 66–73 broke out in Palestine, he retained his loyalty to the family of Roman emperors, beginning with Vespasian in A.D. 69. He died childless in A.D. 100, the last of the Herods.

Vv. 14–22. These verses contain a résumé of the story of Paul's trial before Festus, for the benefit of acquainting Agrippa with the facts concerning the prisoner. Nothing essentially new is given, but the story is given in a dramatic style, and Festus, although unable to understand certain things (vv. 19–20), spoke in a respectful tone.

When Agrippa expressed interest in hearing Paul for himself, Festus agreed. Here is another parallel to Lord's case: He, too, was heard by a Roman governor (Pilate) and a Jewish king (Herod Antipas).

2. Festus presented Paul to the court (25:23–27)

V. 23. The next day the court was convened in the audience hall. Present were Agrippa, Bernice, the five military commanders of Caesarea, and some notable citizens. When they were assembled, Festus commanded that Paul be brought in.

Vv. 24–27. In explaining the essential facts in the case to those (males) present, Festus showed himself to be on the side of Paul, or, at least, on the side of Roman justice. Despite the Jewish accusations against the prisoner, Festus declared, "But I found that he had committed nothing worthy of death."

Festus made clear that he needed to write something to the emperor—possibly those who listened to Paul's defense, especially Agrippa, would be able to suggest a charge of some sort. Almost with a touch of humor Festus noted it seemed absurd to send a prisoner, without any charges against him, to Rome.

3. Paul's defense before the king (26:1–29)

This speech should be compared with the one before the Jewish crowd in chapter 22; one will see the basic similarity in Paul's approach. Yet each speech has its distinctive aspects. While Paul's words, as before, were directed primarily to Jewish ears, he adapted his remarks also to the Gentiles (see vv. 17, 20, 23). Further, "it is one of the most finished passages in the Acts, adorned with rare words, and with an elaboration of style, not to say grandiloquence."[203]

a. Introduction (26:1–3)

After he received permission to speak, Paul presented himself as an orator ("stretched out his hand"). He acknowledged Agrippa as an expert in things Jewish, and begged for a patient hearing (contrast 24:4, where Tertullus spoke before Felix).

b. Paul described his Jewish heritage (26:4–8)

Vv. 4–5. Paul emphasized certain things known to the Jews about his past life; he had lived in Cilicia (cf. 22:3) and then in Jerusalem; he had lived as a Pharisee—the most demanding party among the Jews. Certainly, if the Jews were willing to acknowledge it, he had excellent credentials!

Vv. 6–7. Once again Paul affirmed that he was standing trial because of his belief in the resurrection of the dead. Together, the twelve tribes of Israel hope to attain to that great promise.[204] For this hope, then, he was being accused by Jews! (The form is emphatic, as if to say not by "the Jews," as a distinct group, but by "Jews," of all people—for they certainly believed in the resurrection of the dead.)

V. 8. At this point Paul seems to turn from addressing Agrippa to the Jewish leaders standing near. His question is phrased in the plural ("you") and concerns the central belief of Pharisaism. The implication is clear. God has already raised a man from the dead. That both validates the promise and points to that Man as the Chosen One, the Messiah.

---

203. Rackham, *Acts of the Apostles*, p. 462.

204. This is the earliest known occurrence of the word *dōdekaphylon*, "twelve tribes." It occurs later in Josephus, I Clement, and the Sibylline Oracles. Paul apparently was not aware of any "ten lost tribes"!

c. Paul as a persecutor of the saints (26:9–11)

V. 9. Quite clearly Paul earlier had not believed that Jesus had been raised from the dead. Thus he set out to oppose anyone who related himself to that name (cf. Acts 8:1; 9:1–2; 22:3–4).

Vv. 10–11. Paul took steps to suppress these people: he arrested and jailed many of them; gave his vote[205] for their deaths; punished, harrassed, and pursued them, even in cities outside Palestine (such as Damascus in Syria). He tried to make them blaspheme—to say "Jesus is accursed" (cf. I Cor. 12:3), or in some way to recant by denying their Lord.

d. Paul's heavenly vision (26:12–23)

Once again the narrative of Paul's conversion is given (cf. Acts 9 and 22). Luke included some sayings and descriptions not given in the other accounts.

Vv. 12–14. Armed with his commission from the Sanhedrin, Paul made his way to Damascus. He was struck to the ground at the sight of a light from heaven, and heard a voice calling his name twice "in the Hebrew dialect" (an added detail as compared with 9:4 and 22:7), probably meaning the Aramaic dialect spoken in Palestine. The heavenly voice asserted, "It is hard for you to kick against the goads." This proverb is often taken to mean Paul's conscience had been bothering him, and he should stop fighting against those convicting barbs. It seems preferable to take it as forward-looking: Paul must no longer resist the will of the risen Lord. Johannes Munck[206] adduces much evidence from Greek literature (the words have not been found in any Aramaic source) showing the proverb being related to the folly of resisting the will of God, and interprets, "From now on it will hurt you to kick against the goads, i.e., from now on you will have no discharge from the service that I, Christ, have now laid on you" (cf. I Cor. 9:15–18; Phil. 3:12).

V. 15. This word from the risen Lord must have remained in Paul's mind. How could he be persecuting Jesus? Wasn't He

205. "I cast my vote against them" is literally, "I dropped my black pebble." One voted by using a white pebble for acquittal or a black one for condemnation. Thus we acquired our modern expression *blackballed*.

206. Johannes Munck, *Paul and the Salvation of Mankind* (Richmond: John Knox, 1959), pp. 20–22.

dead? Or, even if He were alive, how could He be affected by Paul's actions? Did Paul then realize that by persecuting the people of the Way he was really persecuting Jesus? This was the germ of his later teaching of the head and the body (the Lord and His church).

Vv. 16–18. Paul was commanded by the Lord to rise, stand, and receive his commission as a minister (one who serves) and a witness (one who tells) of the good news. He would be sent to the Gentiles to bring them from darkness to light, to receive forgiveness and an inheritance by faith in Christ. The language of Paul's commission is indeed reminiscent of certain passages in the prophets, especially in Jeremiah 1:7–8 and Ezekiel 2:1, 3 (and cf. Isa. 42:6–7). His own experience of coming into light (cf. II Cor. 4:6) would be followed by many other being illuminated (cf. Col. 1:12–14). As he wrote his epistle to the churches of Galatia, he recalled how God had called him to preach among the Gentiles (Gal. 1:15–16).

Vv. 19–23. Paul explained to Agrippa that he had spent his days since then declaring to both Jews and Gentiles the need for repentance and conversion (to "turn to God"). He related how the Jews seized him and tried to kill him in Jerusalem. Possibly Agrippa now understood better why Paul had been arrested. It was not simply a question of the resurrection; Paul had also been teaching that Gentiles could come to God on the same level as Jews—both were recipients of His grace.

e. Paul's plea to Festus and Agrippa (26:24–29)

V. 24. Hearing Paul's impassioned words, Festus accused Paul of being insane (as a result of his great learning). He did not appreciate Paul's arguments concerning the decisive character of the Messiah and His ministry.

V. 25. Paul's affirmation of his sobriety (sōphrosynēs) stands opposed to Festus's charge of madness (mania). In Luke 8:38, this soberness of mind is implicitly contrasted with demon possession; in II Corinthians 5:13 it describes the opposite of being "beside oneself." Like his Lord, Paul claimed to speak from God (cf. John 7:17).

Vv. 26–29. In addition, Paul appealed to Agrippa's knowledge of "these matters," the teachings of the prophets about the

Messiah. The coming of Christ into the world had been public; these things did not happen "in a corner."

Then the apostle spoke directly to the king: "Do you believe the prophets?" Agrippa replied, "In a short time you will persuade me to become a Christian." What did he mean by this? If we accept the reading Christianon poiēsai, he meant "to play [a] Christian"; the reading Christianon genesthai means "to become [be] a Christian."[207] The word translated "play," says Haenchen,[208] "in this sense is a technical word of the theatre." Agrippa was not going to be embarrassed by attempting to influence Festus to accept Paul's appeal.

Yet, not discouraged, Paul expressed his deep wish that both the king and all those who heard his words would come to share his faith in Christ. Here is the voice of the evangelist—calling men to receive the light of life.

4. Agrippa and Festus rendered a verdict (26:30–32)

Vv. 30–31. The king and the procurator drew aside and conferred with the leaders of Caesarea. They agreed that Paul deserved neither imprisonment nor death; before Roman law he was innocent.

V. 32. Yet Paul had appealed to Caesar, and that appeal took the decision in the case out of the jurisdiction of Festus. The prisoner must be sent to Rome, and preparations were laid for the voyage.

H. Paul's Voyage to Rome (27:1—28:16)

Once again in Acts, and for the last time, we have a "we" section (in which the writer is included in the narrative). It is striking that Luke gave such a large space to this story of the sea (nearly sixty verses are devoted to it). Two reasons, at least, may be suggested. First, Luke's love for the sea, a characteristic of the Greek mind, shows itself.[209] Second, Luke showed his

---

207. The former reading is found in p[74], Aleph, and Vaticanus (plus others); the latter in the Byzantine text.

208. Haenchen, Acts of the Apostles, p. 689.

209. This is not to say the ancients were unaware of the dangers of the sea. Rackham, Acts of the Apostles, pp. 475–476, has a good discussion of the point.

admiration for the personality of Paul, and he painted in bold strokes the strength of character possessed by his hero (see especially 27:22–26 and 27:31–36).

1. From Caesarea to Crete (27:1–8)

Vv. 1–2. Paul, and other prisoners as well, were put under the care of a centurion named Julius.[210] He was of the Augustan cohort (a troop of the emperor). Some scholars have identified him as one in a corps of couriers involved in communication between the emperor and his military forces; others believe him to have been a legionary centurion. Along with Luke and Paul was Aristarchus of Thessalonica (cf. Acts 19:29; 20:4).

V. 3. When the ship put in to the port of Sidon (in Phoenicia), Julius showed kindness to Paul by allowing him visiting privileges with his friends there.

Vv. 4–8. Putting in at Myra, one of the main grain ports of the Mediterranean, the centurion found an Alexandrian ship bound for Rome, so he had the prisoners transferred to the larger vessel. The voyage became more difficult from this point, for the ship soon put out from the sheltering coastline of Asia Minor, and the strong northwest wind made travel hazardous. Sailing toward the island of Crete, they gained the shelter of the south side at the bay of Fair Havens.

2. From Crete to Malta (27:9–44)

Vv. 9–11. The time for sailing in the open sea was dangerous, for the Day of Atonement (falling in September or October, according to the lunar calendar) was already past. One ancient writer remarked that navigation was dangerous between September 14 until November 11; navigation then ceased until winter had passed.[211] Thus Paul, sensing that loss of life and cargo would result, advised not sailing at present, but the centurion took the word of the pilot and the captain of the ship instead (v. 11).

210. In Luke and Acts, four Roman centurions are referred to: two in the Gospel (7:1–10; 23:47) and two in Acts (10:1ff.; 27:1ff.). They appear as men of sterling character, highly commended.

211. Vegetius, *On Military Affairs* 4.39, cited in Lake and Cadbury, *Beginnings*, IV, 328.

V. 12. As the harbor at Fair Havens was too open to the wind, it was decided by a majority of those on board to sail to Phoenix, another harbor of Crete, and winter there.[212]

Vv. 13–15. When a light wind blew from the south, the crew weighed anchor and began sailing from Fair Havens toward Phoenix (to the west), keeping close to the shore of Crete, just to their starboard side. But suddenly a northeaster bore down upon them—a violent blast of air, literally "a typhonic wind" (typhonikos), driving them into the open sea.

Vv. 16–20. Gaining temporary shelter from the small island of Cauda (modern Gavdho), the sailors were able to haul up the small boat being towed along behind. Then they secured the supporting cables (with which each seagoing vessel was fitted) to protect the hull of the ship, and dropped the sea anchor in order to slow the drift of the ship. Luke said they did this fearing that they eventually might be driven into the great sandbanks (the Syrtis) off the north coast of Africa.

The next day the crew cast the cargo overboard (cf. Jonah 1:5) to lighten the ship. The following day the gear (spare sails and tackle) was put over the side. And as days passed, the storm unabated, everyone (except Paul) gave up all hope of reaching land safely.

Vv. 21–26. At this point Paul stood among the men and spoke a word of encouragement, following upon an "I told you so" (cf. v. 10). Paul urged them to keep up whatever courage they still had, assuring them that no one would lose his life in the storm. As a basis for this amazing forecast, he told them how an angel of God (a God whom he knew and served) had granted him all those on board the ship, and assured him he would indeed stand before Caesar. The ship itself would run aground and be lost to the storm.

Vv. 27–29. Luke resumed the narrative (see v. 20), reporting (certainly from personal recollection) that on the fourteenth day of being blown about in the Adriatic Sea, the sailors became

212. For the problems attending the location of ancient Phoenix, see recent Bible dictionaries or critical commentaries on Acts. Basically, it is a question of relating this name to the port of Lutro (as James Smith had argued), or to modern Phineka (which is now silted up), on which see R. M. Ogilvie, "Phoenix," *Journal of Theological Studies*, N.S., 9, 1958, pp. 308ff.

aware they were approaching land[213] (by the sound of breakers on the shore). Taking soundings, they discovered the water to be about 120 feet deep, then about 90 feet deep. Fearing that the ship might soon be dashed against the rocks, the sailors dropped four anchors from the stern, not only to secure it but also to prevent it from being swung around and presenting a broadside to the waves (as would have happened if they had dropped anchors from the bow).

Vv. 30–32. Surmising what was soon to happen to the ship, the sailors attempted to make their escape in the dinghy, lowering it into the sea under pretense of laying anchors from the bow. Paul, having interpreted their actions, told the centurion that all must stay aboard; otherwise safety would be assured for none. At this, the soldiers cut the ropes, letting the dinghy fall away into the waves.

Vv. 33–35. As the night wore on toward daybreak, Paul kept encouraging the men to eat, for they had had nothing for fourteen days—probably due to their excessive worry for their lives, along with nausea due to the tossing of the ship. Paul gave thanks to God for the food, broke the bread, and took some himself.

Vv. 36–38. The whole group, numbering 276 persons, enjoyed its first meal in two weeks. With renewed strength the crew threw more of the cargo into the sea, preventing the ship from taking on more water.

Vv. 39–41. As the day dawned, the crew observed land beyond them—"a certain bay with a beach." Today this site is known as St. Paul's Bay, and, according to James Smith, "these features still distinguish the coast."[214] Loosing the anchors, freeing the rudders, and hoisting the foresail to gain the wind, the sailors hoped to drive the ship onto the beach. But their plans were thwarted when they struck a channel—the place "where two seas met"—a bank of clay in the middle of the

213. Literally, "some land was approaching them," which James Smith, *The Voyage and Shipwreck of St. Paul* (London: Longmans, Green, & Co., 1880; reprint ed., Baker, 1978), p. 120, calls the "graphic language of seamen."

214. *Ibid.*, p. 141.

entrance to the bay. The prow stuck fast, and the waves beat on the stern, threatening to break up the ship.

Vv. 42–44. To prevent any prisoners from escaping as the ship was broken up by the waves, the soldiers had planned to kill them. Julius, not wanting to see Paul killed, prevented them from carrying out their intention; rather, he commanded all to use their ingenuity to get to land safely. Some could swim; others could float in on anything that would float.

The whole hectic experience was concluded in an almost matter-of-fact way by Luke as he wrote: "And thus it happened that they all were brought safely to land." So Paul's words of assurance (v. 22) and God's promise (v. 24) were fulfilled.

3. From Malta to Rome (28:1–16)

V. 1. Having weathered the storm, the members of the group discovered they had landed on the island of Malta, or Melita (a name meaning "refuge"). Throughout this section of the story the prominence of the pronoun "we" indicates Luke was present with Paul.

Vv. 2–6. The natives of Malta[215] showed great kindness to the group,[216] welcoming these people and kindling a fire to warm them against the cold rain that had set in. When Paul helped to gather wood branches to keep the fire going, he gathered a snake, lying stiff with cold on the ground, along with the wood. Quickly the creature came to life and fastened on Paul's hand, possibly sinking its fangs into him. It seemed evident to the natives that Paul must have been a criminal fleeing from justice, but now Justice (the name of a Greek goddess) had apprehended him!

Quite calmly Paul shook the snake off into the fire.[217] When he showed no ill effects, the natives, after observing for some time, changed their opinion of him, proclaiming him to be a deity (cf. Acts 14:11–12).

215. "Natives" (barbaroi) is, literally, "barbarians." While the natives of Malta were not uncivilized people, Greek writers so described them due to their Phoenician extraction and use of that language.

216. The phrase "they received us all" may refer to the group of Christians (Paul, Luke, and others), rather than all 276 members of the shipwrecked company.

217. Jesus had promised His disciples power over serpents (Luke 10:19), and this incident may be reflected in the closing words of Mark's Gospel (16:18).

Vv. 7–10. The party (the Christians, or the whole group?) was welcomed and entertained by a leading official of Malta, Publius by name. When Paul discovered that his host's father was afflicted with fever and dysentery (a disease common to Malta through the ages), he went in, prayed for the man, laid his hands on him, and healed him. The laying on of hands is frequent in cases of healing in the New Testament (see Mark 5:23; 16:18; Luke 4:40; Acts 9:17).

This incident, when it was known to the inhabitants of the island, resulted in many people coming to Paul and "getting cured." Did Luke assist Paul here by applying his physician's skill? Two things suggest this possibility. First, Luke used two different verbs to describe what happened—*iasato* ("healed") in verse 8, and *etherapeuonto* ("getting cured") in verse 9. Second, the natives' grateful response included both Paul and Luke— "honoured us with many honours" (KJV; v. 10). The word translated "honours" (*timais*) was sometimes used of a physician's fee.[218] Some scholars believe that Luke, in these verses, only "intended to emphasize the very greatness of the miracles which Paul accomplishes."[219]

Vv. 11–15. In this paragraph Luke became very specific in his time notations: "three months . . . three days . . . a day later . . . the second day . . . seven days." Carefully he charted the final days in Paul's approach to the city of Rome.

Paul and Luke sailed from Malta on a ship of the Alexandrian grain fleet which had wintered in the harbor, probably at Valetta. Even the name of the vessel caught Luke's interest; it was called after the Dioscuroi—"the Heavenly Twins"—the twin sons of Zeus, Castor and Pollux. They moved to Syracuse, famous port on the east coast of Sicily, then to Rhegium, and then to Puteoli, the main port of south Italy, located in the Bay of Naples. Here the brethren invited them to stay for seven days, "and thus," wrote Luke—possibly with a memory of exultation and relief— "we came to Rome." As Paul and Luke approached the city, they were met by brethren of the church in Rome at the Appii Forum, a market center about forty-three miles from the city,

218. Compare Ecclesiasticus 38:1, "Honour the doctor for his services" (NEB).
219. Haenchen, *Acts of the Apostles*, p. 715.

and at the Three Inns, located about thirty-three miles from Rome. This warm reception led Paul to give thanks to God for a safe journey and to gain courage. He was not alone as he moved on toward the city!

V. 16. "And when we entered Rome"—Paul's hopes had finally been realized. "I must also see Rome" (19:21); "You must witness at Rome also" (23:11); "I appeal to Caesar . . . to Caesar you shall go" (25:11, 12). Once there Paul was allowed to have private quarters, with the soldier who had been assigned to him and to whom he was chained.

I. Paul's Message to the Jews (28:17–29)

Vv. 17–20 "After three days" in his new situation, Paul called together the leaders (*prōtous*, lit., "the first") of the Jewish communities in Rome. Once more he reiterated his claim that he had done nothing against the Jewish people or the customs of the fathers (cf. Acts 24:14). Yet, he claimed, he was arrested and questioned by the Romans all to no avail—no charge worthy of death was laid against him. Upon his appeal to Caesar he was sent to Rome, and thus he had called these leaders together to plead his case once more. Did he possibly hold a hope that these leaders might be able in some way to vouch for his innocence before Caesar?

Vv. 23–24. A day was agreed upon and the Jews came to Paul's place of lodging. He testified to them of the kingdom of God and spoke of Jesus from the Scriptures ("both the Law of Moses and the Prophets"). These two themes are closely related in Acts (see 1:3; 8:12; 20:24–25; 28:31). The entire Christian proclamation concerning God's presence among mankind (i.e., the kingdom of God) centers in the message concerning the messiahship of Jesus. While Paul's audience listened to him, there was little positive response to the message.

Vv. 25–29. As the hearers were at variance with one another (*asymphōnoi*, lit., "without harmony"), Paul spoke one parting word as the group began to disperse. He affirmed that the Holy Spirit had spoken through Isaiah to their fathers—people just like themselves—who had not listened either. This quotation from Isaiah 6:9–10 had been used also by Jesus against His hearers (see Matt. 13:13–15).

So once again, as Paul had done earlier in Antioch of Pisidia (13:46) and Corinth (18:6), he said he would spend his time preaching to the Gentiles—they would listen to the divine word of salvation.

J. The Apostolic Mission Fulfilled (28:30–31)

V. 30. For two years, at his own expense (for that seems to be the best translation of *misthōmati*, rather than "in his own rented quarters"), Paul carried on, welcoming all who came to visit with him. By the end of this lengthy period his case probably went by default.[220]

V. 31. Notice once again the connection between the kingdom of God and the Lord Jesus Christ. This is a final reminder that this message is for all men—whether Jew, Samaritan, or Gentile.

Amazingly, Paul preached and taught "unhindered" right within the capital of Caesar. The days of government persecution had not yet arrived, but they did begin in A.D. 64, when Nero set fire to Rome and then accused the Christians of the crime.

Thus Luke brought the story of the spread of the gospel to its conclusion. The story began at Jerusalem and concluded at Rome, according to our Lord's commission (Acts 1:8). But the proclamation goes on, and each generation must speak again of the kingdom and the Messiah.

---

220. Bruce, *Acts of the Apostles*, p. 480; and see the lengthy notes in Haenchen, *Acts of the Apostles*, pp. 724–732.

Bibliography

Commentaries

Bruce, F. F. *The Book of the Acts*. Grand Rapids: Eerdmans, 1954.

Foakes Jackson, F. J., and Lake, K., eds. *The Beginnings of Christianity*. Part I: *The Acts of the Apostles*. 5 vols. New York: Macmillan, 1933.

Haenchen, Ernst. *The Acts of the Apostles: A Commentary*. Philadelphia: Westminster, 1971.

Harrison, Everett F. *Acts: The Expanding Church*. Chicago: Moody, 1976.

Kent, Homer A., Jr. *Jerusalem to Rome: Studies in the Book of Acts*. Grand Rapids: Baker, 1972.

Morgan, G. Campbell. *The Acts of the Apostles*. Old Tappan, NJ: Revell, 1924.

Munck, Johannes, ed. *The Acts of the Apostles. Anchor Bible*, vol. 31. New York: Doubleday, 1967.

Rackham, R. B. *The Acts of the Apostles*. London: Methuen, 1901.

Ryrie, Charles C. *The Acts of the Apostles*. Chicago: Moody, 1967.

Vaughan, Curtis. *Acts: A Study Guide Commentary*. Grand Rapids: Zondervan, 1974.

William, C. S. C. *Acts of the Apostles*. New York: Harper and Brothers, 1958.

Background and Reference

Bruce, F. F. *Paul: Apostle of the Heart Set Free*. Grand Rapids: Eerdmans, 1978.

Gettys, Joseph M. *How to Study Acts*. Richmond: John Knox, 1959.

Jewett, Robert. *A Chronology of Paul's Life*. Philadelphia: Fortress, 1979.

Ogg, G. *The Chronology of the Life of Paul*. London: Epworth, 1968.

Ramsay, William M. *St. Paul the Traveller and the Roman Citizen*. Grand Rapids: Baker, 1979. Reprint.

Sandmel, Samuel. *The Genius of Paul*. New York: Farrar, Straus, Cudahy, 1958.

Stendahl, Krister. *Paul Among Jews and Gentiles*. Philadelphia: Fortress, 1976.